Numerology

Self Help Guide of Universe Using Zodiac Signs, Horoscope, Tarot, Enneagram, Kundalini Rising and Empath Healing

(Unlock Self-discovery With Self Esteem for Spiritual Growth)

Nicolas McCants

Published by Rob Miles

© **Nicolas McCants**

All Rights Reserved

Numerology: Self Help Guide of Universe Using Zodiac Signs, Horoscope, Tarot, Enneagram, Kundalini Rising and Empath Healing (Unlock Self-discovery With Self Esteem for Spiritual Growth)

ISBN 978-1-989990-40-7

All rights reserved. No part of this guide may be reproduced in any form without permission in writing from the publisher except in the case of brief quotations embodied in critical articles or reviews.

Legal & Disclaimer

The information contained in this book is not designed to replace or take the place of any form of medicine or professional medical advice. The information in this book has been provided for educational and entertainment purposes only.

The information contained in this book has been compiled from sources deemed reliable, and it is accurate to the best of the Author's knowledge; however, the Author cannot guarantee its accuracy and validity and cannot be held liable for any errors or omissions. Changes are periodically made to this book. You must consult your doctor or get professional medical advice before using any of the suggested remedies, techniques, or information in this book.

Upon using the information contained in this book, you agree to hold harmless the Author from and against any damages, costs, and expenses, including any legal fees potentially resulting from the application of any of the information provided by this guide. This disclaimer applies to any damages or injury caused by the use and application, whether directly or indirectly, of any advice or information presented, whether for breach of contract, tort, negligence, personal injury, criminal intent, or under any other cause of action.

You agree to accept all risks of using the information presented inside this book. You need to consult a professional medical practitioner in order to ensure you are both able and healthy enough to participate in this program.

Table of Contents

INTRODUCTION 1

CHAPTER 1: WHAT IS NUMEROLOGY? 3

CHAPTER 2: KARMIC NUMBERS 6

CHAPTER 3: BASIC MEDITATION TECHNIQUES 14

CHAPTER 4: NUMEROLOGY BASICS 21

CHAPTER 5: THE NINE LAWS OF LEARNING 24

CHAPTER 6: THE COSMIC CLOCK OF TAURUS 33

CHAPTER 7: THE MODERN CONCEPT 54

CHAPTER 8: KARMIC DEBT NUMBERS 57

CHAPTER 9: BEING AT THE RIGHT PLACE AT THE RIGHT TIME 67

CHAPTER 10: FINDING THE LIFE PATH NUMBER 72

CHAPTER 11: THE HIEROPHANT 94

CHAPTER 12: YOUR LUCKY NUMBERS 112

CHAPTER 13: RAGU - URANUS (NUMBER- 4) 122

CHAPTER 14: RECURRING NUMBER 131

CHAPTER 15: THE PHILOSOPHY OF NUMBERS 138

- CHAPTER 16: CAREER ORIENTATION 142
- CHAPTER 17: SUMMARY OF WHAT TO EXPECT FROM YOUR NUMBER 147
- CHAPTER 18: 9 YEAR CYCLE 153
- CHAPTER 19: KARMIC DEFICIT NUMBER: 172
- CHAPTER 20: THE MERCURIAL TEMPERAMENT & ULTIMATE SALESMAN 178
- CHAPTER 21: IF YOU BORN ON THE 7 (SEVENTH) OR 16TH (SIXTEEN OR 25TH (TWENTY FIFTH) OF ANY MONTH THAN KINDLY READ THE FOLLOWING: 185
- CONCLUSION 192

Introduction

Numerology is the study of the meanings of numbers and their relevance to our lives. It can help explain your personality, your abilities, study compatibility in a relationship and predict your future. It allows you to know more about the meaning of your life, understand the different levels of your personality, and identify the why, how, what and when of your relationships.

Traditionally, every object, place or being in the universe has a characteristic vibration, imperceptible to our senses, and that the application of numerology can help to ascertain the vibrations which apply to it, revealing something of its essence.

Two main methods are used in numerology. The first involves converting letters into numbers.

Each letter is associated with a number and the numbers of the letters are added together. If the number is over ten, the digits are added together until there is one digit, (there are a few exceptions to this which are explained below.)

Other methods involve using your date of birth and adding its numbers in a variety of combinations.

The most commonly used techniques of numerology follow the theories of the Greek philosopher and mathematician Pythagoras, who lived in the sixth century BCE. He believed that everything in the universe operates in predictable cycles based on natural law, and that these cycles can be understood through the study of numbers.

Chapter 1: What Is Numerology?

Numerology is an art, which involves the study of numbers and how they reflect on our overall being in respect to a supernatural cosmic plan. The practice dates to over 10,000 years back and evidence shows numerology was used by the ancient Chinese, Japanese, Indians, Egyptians and Babylonians way before it became popular among the Greeks. However, Pythagoras, the Greek mathematician, reinvigorated this system of numbers and is commonly referred to as the father of modern day numerology. According to numerology, each alphabetical letter is assigned a numeric value, which has its own distinct cosmic vibration. There are correlated vibrations produced by the summation of the values assigned to the letters in your name and the summation of the numbers in your date of birth.

What You Will Discover Using Numerology

Numerology will help you discover the following:

*Your talent and abilities; you will discover things you did not know you were capable of doing.

*Your inner mind functions; you will learn how your mind works for you and how to grow and harness its power to enrich your life. You will also learn how your mind changes reality and how it resolves your troubles.

*Who you are and your goals; you will know the direction to follow in life and avoid wasting your energy and time on unimportant matters.

*What others think of you; this includes your friends, family, colleagues, employers, and even your enemies. You may be projecting a totally different image to the outside world from what you think you do. Thus, through numerology, you will learn your true image and how to make it visible to others.

*Your strengths and weaknesses; you will learn what you are good at and what you need to work on.

*How to handle difficult situations; you will learn how to take on threats and difficulties in life. You will know how you respond to stress (rationally, physically, or emotionally). Therefore, you will be equipped on how to use your hidden power to tackle and get rid of stress.

To help you understand better let us now look closely into the numbers and how they are used.

Chapter 2: Karmic Numbers

KARMIC LESSON NUMBERS

Karmic Lesson Numbers show some of the genetic vulnerabilities and unique growth-needed places that have been passed on from your previous lives and need to be tackled in this lifetime. One of the reasons you have decided to incarnate in this present life is to know once and for all and to conquer them. In the event you have a Karmic Lesson Number in your chart of numerology, this karmic lesson will present itself continuously throughout your life until you have worked it out.

Some people have many Karmic Lesson Numbers, and others have none. But if you're lucky enough not to have any, it doesn't mean you're going to have a life that's easy, trouble-free. It simply means that most of your challenges will come through the other numbers in your chart.

HOW TO CALCULATE THE KARMIC LESSON NUMBERS

In a birth certificate name, Karmic Lesson Numbers are derived from the missing numbers between 1 and 9.

If there is any number between 1 and 9, you do not have any karmic lessons; furthermore, every absent number is a Karmic Lesson Number. Let's examine the name of Mary Ann Smith to see if she has some amount of Karmic Lesson Numbers.

M A R Y A N N S M I T H

4 1 9 7 1 5 5 1 4 9 2 8

As you can see, Mary lacks numbers 3 and 6 from her name, so she has a number of 3 Karmic Lessons and a number of 6 Karmic Lessons Number.

The influence of her 3 Karmic Lesson Number is minimized because Mary has a 3 Life Path Number and 3 Current Name Number. Nevertheless, since she has no number 6 among her character figures, in this lifespan, she will have to resolve her 6 Karmic Lesson Number.

KARMIC LESSON NUMBER MEANINGS

Karmic lesson number 1

This lesson shows a need in this life to be more brave, confident, and independent. This experience will encourage you to stand up for yourself, celebrate your independence, and take a path less traveled.

Karmic lesson number 2

This lesson suggests a need for greater cooperation, tolerance, and empathy for others. This experience will encourage you to be more aware of the needs of others, to harmonize with your community, and to learn to work as part of a team.

Karmic lesson number 3

This lesson demonstrates a need for your skills to be more positive and grateful. This lesson will make you lighter, healthier, and faster to go. It will also push you to be less self-critical and life-critical.

Karmic lesson number 4

This lesson shows a need for greater organization, discipline, and focus. This lesson would make you take your commitments seriously and work hard to accomplish your goals. It will also make you responsible and secure.

Karmic lesson number 5

This lesson indicates a need for change to be more open, more flexible, and more hospitable. This lesson will force you to take advantage of your chances and experiences and to be more outgoing and exploratory in life.

Karmic lesson number 6

This lesson shows a need to be more caring, diligent, and honest to others and life. This lesson will force you to take your obligations seriously and build true and meaningful relationships with others.

Karmic lesson number 7

This lesson indicates a need for the discovery of the deeper meaning of life to look beyond the physical world. This lesson will force you to have more confidence in yourself and others. It will encourage you to be open-minded and find a spiritual belief.

Karmic lesson number 8

This lesson is an indication of the need to reclaim personal power over anything that discourages you. This lesson should compel you to understand money, status, power, and authority. It will help you to learn how to deal with your material problems.

Karmic lesson number 9

This lesson advocates a need to be more understanding, tolerant, and less judgmental of others. This lesson will force you to learn to forgive and broaden your understanding of others and of life.

KARMIC DEBT NUMBERS

If in your seven Personality Numbers, you have a 13/4, 14/5, 16/7, or 19/1, it is considered a Karmic Debt Number. Karmic Debt Numbers indicate particular lessons to be mastered in this lifetime because in previous lives we have not learned them. Each amount of Karmic Debt has its own special lessons and burdens. Let's look at what they are:

Karmic Debt number 13/4

This number shows that extra effort is needed in this lifetime to master discipline, integrity, and determination. You need to strive to be proactive and tackle the problems head-on rather than resort to quick fixes, excuses, and intimidation with a 13/4 in your character numbers. Karmic Debt Number 13/4 provides an opportunity for personal transformation, and you will overcome this lesson when you are honest, patient, and persevere through adversity.

Karmic Debt number 14/5

This number indicates that you need to show sobriety and moderation in every area of your life and be aware of gluttony. You must learn to rise above temptation and earthly desires with a 14/5 among your personality numbers in favor of accountability and honoring your promises. You are going to overcome this lesson by balancing your desire for freedom and adventure with your responsibilities.

Karmic Debt number 16/7

This number indicates a need to reassess your core values and remove any surface foundations that do not align with your higher self. You should strive to climb above your ego and pride with a 16/7 in your character numbers, treat others with respect, trust and yield to the unexpected events of your existence, and be honest and true in love. You will overcome this lesson by focusing on your personal development and rising above your artificial tendencies.

Karmic Debt number 19/1

This number shows a sense of anger because of the inability to control everything and everybody in your life. With a 19/1 in the Personality Numbers, you need to learn to take into account the desires, thoughts, and views of others rather than your own. You will resolve this experience by having the courage to accept help from others, acknowledging your faults, and seeing the opinions of others (regardless of whether they are right or wrong).

Chapter 3: Basic Meditation Techniques

Meditation is an ancient technique found in nearly every religious tradition – big or small – and in every culture throughout history. It can remove stress, create calm and is recognized as a treatment for depression, anxiety and many related disorders by doctors and the medical establishments in many different countries. The full health benefits of meditation have not been fully researched but medical experts agree that it can not only help with mental health but be beneficial for many physical conditions and is even a natural pain killer!

Meditating with crystals is the perfect way to not only program the crystals themselves but also to focus your own mind on a specific goal. Depending on your intentions or needs, you should choose an appropriate crystal for the meditation (see the section on types of crystals later in this book). In this chapter we'll take a look at basic meditations that can be used as a framework to meditate with crystals and can be adapted for different purposes.

Meditation Basics

Always meditate in a quiet space, where you will not be interrupted. Some people choose to meditate with candles, incense or music and all of these can be helpful in achieving a state of relaxation. Choose which, if any, works for you and try different methods until you find the most effective "tools".

Wear loose fitting clothing (or none at all) and ensure that the room (or space) is at a comfortable heat. As you meditate your body's processes will slow and you may feel colder.

Remaining physically comfortable is important when meditating; you can meditate for a few moments or much longer, especially as you practice, so minimizing any possible distractions, including physical ones, is essential.

After meditating it can be important to bring yourself firmly back into the real world. Have a hot drink and snack, play some louder music, go for a walk in the fresh air and sunlight (or wind and rain!). Ground yourself back in the real world in whatever way suits you best.

Basic Mindfulness Meditation

Mindfulness is a meditation technique that has roots in Buddhist practice and it is one of the most common meditation techniques used today. Mindfulness meditation can be conducted anywhere, anytime and is a way of simply relaxing and fully experiencing the moment. You can practice mindfulness meditation at home, work or in the park (though be sure to practice relaxation techniques in a safe place). It's a good type of meditation for those learning to meditate and will help you to develop your skills in order to be able to conduct deeper, more effective forms of meditation. The following basic mindfulness meditation can last for as long, or short, a period as you require.

1. Focus your attention on the moment; stand or sit upright and close your eyes.

2. Ask yourself "what am I experiencing right now? What thoughts, what feelings, what physical sensations?"

3. Acknowledge each thought, emotion, sensation, good and bad alike.

4. Gradually redirect your attention to your breathing. Simply focus on the sensation of the air entering your lungs and leaving your lungs. Breath in through your nose and out through your mouth.

5. Allow your sense of awareness to expand once more, to each physical sensation, sounds and your own presence in the space in which you are meditating. Continue to breath regularly and deeply.

6. As thoughts surface, note them and move on. Do not allow one thought to

distract you but continue to focus on the present, physical moment.

7. Conclude by stretching, yawning, taking a deep breath in and opening your eyes as you expel the air from your lungs.

Pyramid Meditation

This meditation will help you to learn to visualize – an important part of meditation, healing and crystal healing. Use it to practice and develop both your meditation skills and your crystal healing skills.

1. Hold your crystal in either hand – whichever feels "right" and sit on the floor in a cross legged position.

2. Close your eyes and take three deep breaths, breathing in through the nose and filling the lungs. Hold each breath to the count of three. Expel the air from your lungs in a short breath through your mouth. Repeat this process two more times. You may feel a little lightheaded but this is normal.

3. Count backwards from nine to one taking a breath at each number. Do this slowly and rhythmically and as you do so remind yourself to return to full consciousness in ten or fifteen minutes. Your mind and internal body clock should do this automatically but if you prefer you can set an alarm.

4. Continue to breath at the rate you have established in step three and with your eyes closed begin to focus on the color associated with your aims. This should be the same color as the crystal you are using.

5. Visually, in your mind, construct a pyramid, with the tip located a foot or so above your head. The four points should fall on the floor around you, two behind and two in front. Imagine the color flooding this pyramid.

6. If you are using the meditation for healing, feel the color washing around you within the pyramid and focus it towards

the area you wish to heal, or the source of pain.

7. Towards the end of the session, either when your own internal alarm begins to bring you back to fuller consciousness or the alarm you have set rings, simply focus on your breathing and count back from one to nine and open your eyes at nine.

8. Visually imagine the pyramid dissolve around you and focus for a moment or two on the crystal in your hand. Once you feel you have fully returned to consciousness end the meditation and ground yourself back in the real world.

Chapter 4: Numerology Basics

Numerology is one of the oldest ways to study numbers. Yet, since it is practiced in different parts of the world, there are various approaches used to calculate numbers, and each strategy may vary depending on the tradition of the person who is practicing the method. The fundamentals of numerology is not special as most may think, but it is the best way for you to determine on how things work with numerology and how numerologists arrive on their calculations.

A Little Background About Numerology

The whole concept of numerology started when Pythagoras, the father of geometry, connect everything to numbers. He even stated that each person has thier own specific personality and unique vibration. Pythagoras is also the one who divided the soul of humans into nine types, and these numbers are still used in modern society. Numerology is concerned on nothing but numbers. It mainly concentrates on the numbers 1 to 9 in which some numbers are reduced. In numerology, zero is not considered as a number. It adds nothing to any digits. The number 10 exists as number one's composite.

The Art of Numerology

The best thing about numerology is that anyone can be a numerologist. The only thing you need is paper, pen, and some calculations. Numerology, when compared to some divination methods, constantly moves and uses the magnetic energy of the earth. Since the soul is just one of the parts of the universe, the numbers are symbols which would help you translate the world around you. Each person has several numbers which can work as codes. If these numbers were deciphered, you will learn about destiny, karma, spiritual, emotional, and personality influences. You will even discover why there are people who get on your nerves and how you can figure it out.

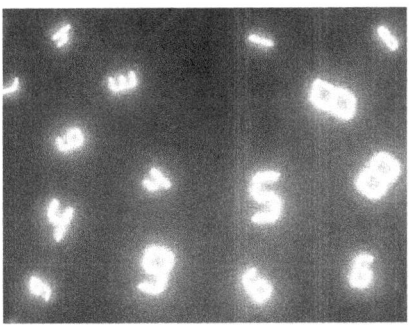

Chapter 5: The Nine Laws Of Learning

1: The Law of Experience

Have you heard the proverb, "Don't judge a man until you've walked a mile in his shoes?" Or the modern expression, "You know my name but not my story?" The Law of Experience encourages you to go out in the world and confront life firsthand to get an authentic feel of what you desire to go through physically, emotionally, and spiritually. It teaches you to quickly recognize what you like and what you hate; and it propels you towards what you know will definitely make you grow. Determine what you want to experience and make a run for it. Notice how good it feels whenever you mentally tell yourself, "Been there done that!" Endeavor to engage your learning with purpose and walk the talk until the very end. When you align with The Law Of Experience, you develop your sense of achievement and shape your individuality.

2: The Law of Anticipation

The Law of Anticipation encourages you to align with your sensitivity and intuition. When you focus more on your gut feeling and start paying attention to what feels right, you allow the natural occurrence of life to steer you towards the right type of learning that is made just for you. Prevent yourself from becoming overwhelmed by your thinking mind by practicing breathing techniques; do some yoga; or follow up your workout session with meditation and allow yourself to become familiar with your intuitive mindset. Train this habit and your gut feeling will surely become an adept at attracting all the right learning at the right time. When you align with The Law Of Anticipation, you turn down what doesn't feel right and let your inner voice say yes to the things that do.

3: The Law of Playfulness

For your mind to execute something well, it must be void of all concerns. Concerns and worries dismantle the fun in anything, especially in learning. Have you ever noticed how good you are when you just wing it without giving it a single thought? This is because you actually allow your mind to focus on the execution of the action rather than telling it to analyze the action, which is counter-productive. Before you do anything, close your eyes and visualize yourself excelling at what you are about to learn. Most importantly, see yourself having fun doing it. Fun prevents nervousness and stress which are the killers to a sound and functional brain. Notice how your body feels right now and allow the tension around your shoulders to ease and disappear. Take a deep breath and remind yourself that life is your own playground. Now wear a confident smile and wing it. When you align with The Law Of Playfulness, your mind becomes more curious and creative during the learning curve; as this becomes your habit, allow yourself to be amazed at how much fun you can have each time you experience new learning.

4: The Law of Repetition

Have you ever heard the saying, "Practice makes perfect?" The Law Of Repetition encourages the traditional route of learning. There is a reason why we were all taught as children to learn through repetition: because it works. It is said that the average person needs twenty-one days until what they are learning becomes part of their long-term memory. Whenever you tackle learning through repetition, diligence is the key to your success. So before you sit down to learn, plan what you will be doing. Organize the area and take away any potential distraction. By knowing exactly what you will do from A to Z, your mind is less likely to become overwhelmed and discouraged. When you align with The law Of Repetition, avoid daydreaming as you need to focus your mind strictly on understanding the mechanics of your routine. When you make this into your habit, you cultivate a more down-to-earth character and develop reliability.

5: The Law of Exhaustion

Sometimes, you just know when you haven't done enough or given your one hundred percent. The Law Of Exhaustion speaks of committing all five senses to your learning. To learn something and do it properly, you must be willing to forget the notion of time and throw yourself off the bridge, so to speak. Be there in energy and presence and exhaust yourself in the process. If you hold back, it will be like starting a workout regime half-heartedly and going only half way through… just because you didn't feel it. The key here is to end up feeling completely depleted mentally, physically, or emotionally. Once you have exceeded yourself, stop and be amazed at how much you have learned. Make it your new habit to push yourself beyond your comfort zone. When you align with The Law Of Exhaustion, you get used to taking more risks and that allows you to outgrow your limitations.

6: The Law of Comfort

It is never comfortable when you learn something new. It defies your existing values and challenges what you believe in. It stretches you away from your mental comfort zone and induces fear. Your mind then finds reasons to validate your objection to learning. Set your level of mental satisfaction higher than what your mind is used to. Crave learning as you would crave for food and become satisfied only after you have put in some work. Find new creative ways to become comfortable while you are learning so you can minimize the disruption of peace in mind, heart, and body. When you aligned with The Law Of Comfort, you naturally know how to make yourself at home, no matter where learning takes place.

7: The Law of Precision

To know something well is to know it with precision. That is when The Law Of Precision comes into play. Learning what you are taught alone is not enough. Make it a habit for your mind to connect the dots. Go out of your way to dig for information below the surface level and use what you understand to improve your learning ability. Explore the five W's: who, what, why, when, where, and how. Conduct research from every angle until you know everything with precision. As you do these things, you naturally strengthen your critical thinking skills. When you align with The Law Of Precision, you give yourself the right tools to become a true specialist of your chosen field.

8: The Law of Choosing

In order to reap the benefits of learning, first recognize what is worth your time. But before that, become aware of what makes you unique. The Law of Choosing speaks of recognition and the importance of giving yourself credit. Sit down with a pen and paper and list ten things that make you great. Know this to prevent yourself from settling for less than you deserve. To make use of what you have is the most important piece of advice to truly experience this law. You are guaranteed to get what you know you deserve by first experiencing things that you think you deserve. If you do not know what you deserve, then simply experience what you know will be good for you in the long run. Do this for a month or two and assess whether or not what you are doing is worth maintaining. If the choices you made are not empowering you in any way, stop everything, change gears and start in a new direction. When you align with The Law of Choosing, you strengthen self-love, cultivate ambition, and allow yourself to get in touch with your will power.

9: The Law of Trust

Through this law, you are asked to let go of all the reasons why you think it cannot be done. Awaken to your ideals. Allow yourself to trust the process until completion. Dare to be unrealistic and visualize within your mind's eye your desired outcome. Imagine what it feels like to succeed. Make it a habit to tune into your positive mindset for at least five minutes every morning when you wake up. Trust that your vision is real and simply be expectant during the learning process. When you align with The Law of Trust, you strengthen your sense of hope and develop belief, much needed in times when learning becomes a burden.

Chapter 6: The Cosmic Clock Of Taurus

The function of the Cosmic Clock is to show the position of the sun in the Zodiac each month and its influence on Taurus. Example: Taurus is bothered in August with problems concerning dwelling, home, and family. It can be seen in the Cosmic Clock that the reason for this is the sun in the 4th house (Leo). Taurus will feel relief in September when the sun moves into the 5th house (Virgo.)

Taurus' Monthly Forecast

Taurus

Gemini

Cancer		
Leo		
Virgo		
Libra		
Scorpio		
Sagittarius	Capricorn Aquarius	Pisces
Aries		
April 20	–	May 20
May 21	–	June 20
June 21	–	July 22
July 23	–	August 22
August 23 – September 22		September 23 – October 22
October 23 – November 21		November 22 – December 20
Sun in the 8th house		
December 21 – January 20		January 21 – February 19
February 20 – March 19		March 20 – April 19
Sun in the 9th house	Sun in the 10th house	Sun in the 11th house
Sun in the 12th house	Sun in the 1st house	Sun in the 2nd house
Sun in the 3rd house	Sun in the 4th house	Sun in the 5th house
Sun in the 6th house	Sun in the 7th house	

Note: See chapter on the monthly forecast to obtain the characteristics and meanings of the 12 houses of the Cosmic Clock.

Taurus: Relationships with Other Signs

Taurus 1st house Gemini 2nd house Cancer 3rd house Leo 4th house Virgo 5th house Libra 6th house Scorpio 7th house Sagittarius 8th house Capricorn 9th house Aquarius 10th house Pisces 11th house Aries 12th house

Example: Taurus will be rewarded with warmth and love in the company of Virgo, but may feel vulnerable and offended by Sagittarius.

GEMINI – MAY 21st to JUNE 20th

The key word for Gemini is NEXT! They are easily bored and want to get ahead quickly. Mobility, movement, communication, change, and variation are the central features of this sign. One can assume that Capricorn and Virgo would get dizzy next to Gemini; since Gemini is capable of talking on the phone (an obsession with this sign!), shouting and waving at friends outside the window, nursing the baby, getting a beer out of the fridge, and writing a note about what to do tomorrow all at the same time. This is nothing compared to their physical coordination and their ability to do everything piece by piece.

Gemini would sell ice to Eskimos and convince them that it's colder, cheaper, and more usable ice. In short, Gemini is an expert salesperson. In addition, they can be campaigners, marketing representatives, copyrighters, advertising agents, and can do anything it takes to sway and convince an audience. A jack of all trades.

Gemini is youthful in build and behavior: he talks a lot but does not always mean what he says. Incidentally, this is also a reason why George Bush, a Gemini, said, "Read my lips. I will not raise taxes" and then forgot he said it, thus ceding the oval office to Bill Clinton, a roaring Leo. The Don Juan side of the Gemini is well represented by John F. Kennedy, who was young, verbal, and won the famous televised debate in 1960 against the ashy Capricorn Richard Nixon. It is now known that Kennedy had a connection with Marilyn Monroe, also Gemini, who was beautiful, sexy, and complicated as only a Gemini can be inside.

The ease of communication toward the outside hides the inner, chaotic, complex and troubled soul of the Gemini. Actress Mio Mio, who played a call girl, is a Gemini, and the duality is reflected in her stage name. Actor Michael J. Fox, born June 9th, has always appeared much younger than he is. He is known to suffer from Parkinson's disease, an affliction associated with Gemini.

Remember that Gemini has mystical connections to a mythological group called the Puare Eternus — always young. Kennedy, Fox, even Bob Hope, Brooke

Shields and Paul McCartney are well-known Geminis, forever young in spirit and appearance. McCartney, by the way, worked for the Royal Mail before he became a Beatle (the postal service is connected with Gemini), and since duality is an attribute, he also had a partner – named John Lennon.

Whoever would like to understand the typical Gemini should see the movie "Good Morning, Vietnam," in which Robin Williams (a Leo, by the way) as a crazed radio D.J. portrays the role of the Gemini to excellence. Words, words, they once sang. Pe-ro-le, pe-ro-le, pe-ro-le… He said – but did he mean it? Someone already came up with the typical Gemini-Mercury proverb in the U.S. during the 1950's: "I do not care what you write about me as long as you spell my name right…" The media and the talk show are the Gemini's story – the world ends as soon as they run out of words. This is in contrast to the Pisces, where the curtain goes up as soon as they stop talking. Incidentally, they feel "wonderful" together, since one broadcasts on F.M. and the other on A.M., or perhaps and more correct – one on continuous broadcast and the other on silent radio.

Conception of Time – Gemini views the dimension of time as an economic resource, and for some reason, at certain stages is forced to steal or manipulate it. He will find himself emotionally drained, guilt-laden, and labeled with regard to time, and can also create a distortion of time. This happens because Capricorn occupies Scorpio's 8th house and makes things difficult. There could be a penchant for tolling clocks, by the way. With Gemini, there could be loss or forgetting of time or, in contrast, an obsession with time. A strange paradox, as Pisces in the 10th house dissolves the dimension of time. Denial mechanisms are possible in relation to age and time, along with attempts to erase time lines through certain professions.

Career and Work – Scorpio occupies Gemini's 6th house, and therefore, Gemini may find himself in an occupation involving secrecy or finance, deep-sea diving or psychology, medicine or therapeutic areas. There is something obsessive about work, and they experience cycles of destruction, formation, and reconstruction in relation to professions. Gemini knows how to turn a partnership into a force.

They will feel cheated and betrayed, and will often be forced into competition. Jealousy and sex may be associated with work. Since Gemini is typically suited for journalism or television interviews, Scorpio in the 6th house can turn the interview into an intensive investigation, typified by Barbara Walters, in which the guest is cajoled into revealing what he didn't wish to divulge, upping the rating points of the show. The bottom line –

Scorpio money. Money and work are sensitive issues with Gemini. Oprah Winfrey proves the point completely. (Incidentally, Oprah herself is an Aquarius.)

Since Pisces occupies the 10th house of careers, Gemini will experience situations of emptiness and dissolution with respect to careers or will feel victimized. (For Kennedy and Marilyn Monroe, these scripts have played out many times – from sex to Scorpio-style death.)

Because of their work or roles, and against their nature, Geminis will often be required to identify deeply on an emotional level with individuals. Israeli President, Ezer Weitzman, a Gemini, is frequently found in homes comforting bereaved families in times of loss, in contrast to his former image as an arrogant pilot. Gemini is also involved in music, song and poetry, creative endeavors, and therapy. Feelings of isolation, lack of communication, and disappointment are experienced in connection with work. Gemini professions include transportation, commerce, marketing, advertising, public relations, brokering, education, counseling, and communications.

Money – Gemini has monetary connections to the past and to history, as well as to the home, the family, and the mother figure. They profit through work and mature characters, but also through secret dealings and manipulation or brokering of real estate. Older Geminis will receive inheritance. Money is also obtained from insurance and in connection with health. Financial losses are possible, and Gemini should be cautious with respect to real estate and land issues.

Gemini can also earn a living and profit from criticism and instruction, education, counseling and guidance; and of course, communications and commercial enterprise, including motor vehicles.

Illusions and irrationality in connection with money can occur. There is a somewhat fatalistic streak involving money and resources.

Communication and Thought – Gemini is a logical thinker with excellent ability for expression and handling of information, both with regard to gathering and disseminating. There are unconventional thoughts, original ideas, and even inventive abilities with an eye on the future. Brainstorms and inventions are associated with travel abroad, but are usually all talk and little action. The position of Leo in the 3rd house indicates the ability for public relations and marketing, an example being George Bush's "marketing" of the Gulf War.

Relationships and Sexuality – Beauty and esthetics are of prime importance for Gemini. This is the chief criterion for falling in love and choosing a mate. Gemini marries for love, and there could be harmony, as Libra occupies the 5th house.

We must add, however, that Leo in the 3rd house could create duality in the love relationship. This quality is further strengthened by the open, carefree, adventurous, and curious Sagittarius in the 7th house, which fosters acquaintance during academic studies, short journeys, or travel abroad.

Relationships have elements of humor as well as freedom, adventure, and experimentation: what's waiting for us beyond the horizon. Gemini bores easily and it is important that the partner be communicative, youthful, intelligent, and even a bit aristocratic. (Very few demands, it seems………)

Gemini's partner may be employed in law, creative pursuits, acting, sports, or academics. Gemini wants to "win the lottery" through the life partner. The motivation of mobility and searching, change and variation is a connection to love and marriage. Gemini is also a matchmaker.

On a sexual level there is something of a rational nature, which includes sexual connections to an older adult or authority figure, or intimate liasons associated with work or career. In spite of Gemini's powerful sexuality, there can be long periods of limitations, restrictions, and deprivations in the areas of sex, warmth, and physical affection. Gemini is critical and judgmental of the partner, with a tendency toward control. There is a need to heal and to be healed with respect to sexuality. It is interesting to note that Dr. Ruth Westheimer, the famous sexual therapist and author, is a Gemini. Children – Attractive, creative, intelligent, talented, but not calm; tall, social, possessing abilities to improvise and to invent; friendly, surprising and often amazing; nervous energy, constant motion, and sportive are typical characteristics. There may be the birth of twins. Gemini possesses a great love for children through communication and speaking rather than deep emotional expression; he reaches their intellect.

Home and family – The home is a place of criticism and education to perfection, intellectual pursuit, cleanliness, and order. The father is associated more with these qualities, while the mother is more physical and persistent, and may involve feelings of sacrifice and victimization. There is something obsessive regarding the dependence on the parental images and the necessity for mutual sacrifice. The parents may have health problems or Gemini may experience the loss of a parent or older figure (Capricorn in the 8th house). There is complexity and difficulty in relation to the mother image.

Siblings are active, dynamic, boastful, and talented; and the connection wavers from love to rivalry and occasionally aggression. They may be associated with advertising, creative enterprise, work with children and youth, perhaps acting and direction.

Legal situations – With Sagittarius in the 7th house, legal situations may involve marital relationships, partners, or partnerships but also possible are lawsuits in connection with money at work, bosses, authority figures, or intimate sex scandals. There also may be a legal connection with regard to studies, sports, or travel abroad.

Health – Sensitivity may exists in several areas, including the respiratory tract and lungs, the nervous system, ears, vocal cords, throat, nose, thyroid, the metabolic system, hands, shoulders, the urinary tract, and sexual organs.

Sports, Travel, Social Life, and Studies – Sudden, unplanned trips abroad may occur as well as separation or disconnection from studies. Gemini loves team sports and sports connected with aviation.

Gemini has a very liberal view of the world, future-oriented and open-minded. There can be connections with group activities abroad of a humanitarian nature during the course of his life.

Gemini generally does not obligate himself to his friends, preferring relationships with more openness and freedom. He is stimulated by social occasions and unusual, special individuals. Gemini is inclined to be selfish on a social level, and friends are likely to be younger than he is, although he aspires to be one with the aristocratic set. Latent and secret are desires for control and authority as well as a well-disguised drive to manipulate.

Difficulties and Emotional Stumbling Blocks – The area of money and finance is a source for poor judgment, victimization, and self-destruction; and there may be hidden enemies. Taurus in the 12th house is the source of this, as Gemini lacks stability and territory. He yearns for this, but he has a hard time defining his exact station in life. Incidentally, Taurus in the 12th house is enough of a reason that many Geminis are involved in music, song-writing, and poetry; but let us not forget that Pisces occupies the 10th house of careers for Gemini. Taurus in the "Piscean" 12th house indicates a decline in the Taurus' gravitational effect (perhaps even a total lack of it…). Capricorn in the 8th house strengthens this with the idea that the only thing certain is change and constant transformation. A life without static.

Gemini either has no habits or routines or else he is addicted to destructive bad habits. He can develop dependency relationships with authority figures or older individuals, perhaps in connection with family, work, or career. He can go through cycles of destruction and re-building. He has inhibitions and problems in demonstrating deep emotions and empathy, which can be tied to an ulterior motive – Pisces in the 10th house.

Mode of Dress – Freestyle, sportive, and youthful, extroverted, attentiongetting and stands out in a crowd. Gemini loves imported clothing, with Sagittarius in the 7th house and Libra in the 5th.

Relationship to the Past and the Future — The past is connected with criticism, money, practicality, perfection, and treatment, especially in relation to the home and family. Gemini has a great love of the future, which is conceptualized as a gamble, full of freedom, new developments, and new thought channels — an open expanse of limitless possibilities.

Religion — To the outside, Gemini is open-minded and easy-going. Inside, he experiences vulnerability, worry, and suspicion in this area; a concealed fear that the Lord sees and knows all. Mostly, the view is one of secular liberalism.

Death — Gemini's relationship to death is rational and cold. There is a connection between the idea of death and that of work and career. In any event, the prevailing idea is that there is no need to think too much about something that will occur regardless. The connection between death and career is expressed by the journalists and writers located in remote corners of the globe and covering hostilities and violence. The communicative Gemini is interested in revealing maximum information about a particular place or circumstance, often risking death in obtaining the story.

Gemini is able to demand or supply an ultimatum in situations connected with money, sex, or mature figures. For some reason, there is also an association of health and medicine to death. Relationships of criticism, rationality, fatalism, feelings of guilt, and the sensation that death is a divine fate are common to Gemini.

Army – Gemini aspires to freedom and independence in the army. He will gain many new friends and acquaintances during service, but there will also be periods of disconnection and separation. Surprises are to be expected in duties involving contacts with many people and groups or innovations in technology and computers. It is likely that service may involve the Air Force, given that the military Aries is located in the 11th house of Aquarius. Gemini displays great abilities for improvisation and originality in the army. In addition, the army is associated with the processing of information 24-hours a day, which is of interest to Gemini.

Environment and Neighbors – Gemini often displays pride, showiness, and arrogance but also warmth and love; at the same time selfishness and aggression along with fatherly leadership. There might be a famous or creative neighbor, younger neighbors, or athletes nearby.

Cars – With Leo occupying the 3rd house, Gemini desires a luxury car that stands out and makes a distinct impression on all those around. He loves to drive as fast as allowed, and if possible, he would turn his car into an aircraft.

Sacrifices, Confusions, Illusions, and Places Where it is Difficult to be Rational and Objective – As strange as it may seem, there are situations of sacrifice and victimization. Failures, denial mechanisms, confusion, and illusion could take place in relation to older figures, parents, or authorities. There are sensations of time sacrificed in relation to an unattained goal. Loss, confusion, and errors may be associated with property and possessions, money, or real estate. Illusions and feelings of missing out are connected to careers. Gemini will be forced to display empathy and sacrifice in his career, against his nature; and will have difficulty detaching himself from these situations.

Chapter 7: The Modern Concept

For the most part, numerology can be summed up as any study that includes investigation into the divine or mystical in regards to the relationship to numbers therein. Although Numerology itself comes in many forms, depending on the area it originated from, the basic concepts for reach number are always pretty much the same. In addition, what was formerly known as the scientific study "isopsephy" among ancient mathematicians like our man, Pythagoras, is now merely considered pseudo-mathematics and/or pseudoscience by the modern scientific and mathematic communities.

Interestingly, numerology has a strong yet idyllic association with astrology, paranormal studies, and even divination. However, the word "numerology" is typically used as a derogatory term for people who believe it. Unfortunately, many ignorant people assume that numerology followers have an excess reliance to the numerical patterns associated with it; and what's more, those who believe this way are seldom willing to learn the basics in order to decide for themselves. In fact, the term for this supposed pseudoscience, "numerology," was not even coined until the early 1900s, by which time the vast majority of society had dismissed its importance.

What we now know in the western world as "numerology" has been changed over the centuries, although the same basic principles still permeate the belief systems. There are numerous ancient societies, cultures, and teachers who have had influence on the practice of numerology throughout history: Babylonia, Greece, Hellenistic Alexandria, early Christian mystics, teachers of the Kabala and the Hindu Vedas, practitioners of the Egyptian Book of the Dead, and several others. With so many insights coming from so many societies and points in history, it certainly begs the question as to why numerology is not a more widely practiced art by the mainstream.

Chapter 8: Karmic Debt Numbers

Numerology is based on the ancient idea that each of us is a spiritual being who incarnates on the earth to further evolve toward higher states of awareness.

During our long evolutionary path, we have accumulated a wealth of wisdom, and have made many positive choices that benefit us in the future. We have also made mistakes, and have sometimes abused the gifts we have been given. To rectify such errors, we may take on an additional burden in order to learn a particular lesson that we failed to learn previously. In numerology, this burden is called a Karmic Debt.

The numbers that indicate a Karmic Debt are 13, 14, 16, and 19. These double-digit numbers take on great significance when they are found in the core numbers (the most important numbers including the Life Path, Expression, Heart's Desire (or Soul

Urge), Personality, and Birth Day), and in the various cycles during the course of your lifetime. Each has its own unique characteristics, and its own particular difficulties.

When you are calculating your chart - especially you core numbers and different cycles - you may encounter the numbers 1, 4, 5, or 7. These single-digit numbers can be arrived at by adding a variety of two-digit numbers. The number 1 can be arrived at, for example, by combining the double-digit numbers of 10 (1 + 0 = 1), 19, 28, 37, 46 - all of which total to 10, and then to 1. However, only in the case of 19 is a Karmic Debt indicated. Karmic Debts are also associated with the numbers 4, 5, and 7.

Karmic Debt numbers can be preceded by an array of two-digit numbers, but when the 4 is preceded by a 13; or when the 5 is preceded by a 14; or the 7 by a 16; a Karmic Debt is also read as part of the single-digit interpretation.

A Karmic Debt can be found in different places in the chart. As a result of totals based on your date of birth, for instance, or calculations based on the letters of your name. This means that two people with a 16 Karmic Debt that is located in different places in the chart, express it very differently. Thus, all I can do is lay out the general characteristics of the Karmic Debt, and some broad guidelines for dealing with it.

KARMIC DEBT NUMBER 13

Those with the 13 Karmic Debt will work very hard to accomplish any task. Obstacles stand in their way, and must be overcome time and again. One may often feel burdened and frustrated by the seeming futility of one's efforts there may be a desire to surrender to the difficulties and simply give up on the goal, believing it was impossible to attain in the first place. Some with the 13 Karmic Debt fall to laziness and negativity. But efforts are not futile, and success is well within reach.

One simply must work hard, and persevere in order to reach the goal. Many highly successful people in all walks of life, including business, art, and athletics, have a 13 Karmic Debt.

The key to succeeding with the 13 is focus. Very often, people with the 13 Karmic Debt do not concentrate or direct their energies in one specific direction, or on a single task, but scatter their energies over many projects and jobs, none of which amount to very much. A temptation with the 13 is to take shortcuts for quick success. Too often, that easy success doesn't come, causing regret and the desire to give up. The result is a poor self-image, and the belief that one is incapable of amounting to very much.

In order to focus, you must maintain order in your life. Order is essential to success. You must maintain a schedule, keep appointments, and follow through. Keep your environment neat and under control, and never procrastinate. If you sustain a steady and consistent effort, you will realize much reward.

KARMIC DEBT NUMBER 14

The 14 Karmic Debt arises from previous lifetimes during which human freedom has been abused. Those with a 14 Karmic Debt are forced to adapt to ever-changing circumstances and unexpected occurrences. There is an acute danger of falling victim to abuse of drugs, alcohol, and overindulgence in sensual pleasures, such as food and sex. You must put the reins on yourself. Modesty in all affairs is crucial to overcoming this Karmic Debt.

Also important is the need to maintain order in life, and to establish one's own emotional stability. you must also be willing to adapt to the unexpected occurrences of life, all the while maintaining your focus on your goals and dreams. Flexibility and adaptability are at the very core of this struggle. Orderliness in one's immediate environment is crucial to maintaining clarity and focus. Mental and emotional stability must be attained in order to avoid being thrown about by the changing fortunes in the external environment.

But the key to the 14 Karmic Debt is commitment. Life will resemble a roller coaster ride, but it will always travel in the right direction if one's heart is set on what is true and good. Set yourself a high goal, maintain order wherever possible in your life, avoid excessive sensory indulgence, and maintain faith. Above all, do not give up on your dreams and goals. Those with the 14 Karmic Debt will experience life to the fullest, and as long as they maintain a high dream, they will achieve success and great spiritual development.

KARMIC DEBT NUMBER 16

The 16 Karmic Debt - wherever it shows up on the chart - means destruction of the old and birth of the new. The 16 is about the fall of the ego, and all that it has built for itself. It is a watershed, a cleansing. All that has been constructed, and all that serves to separate the person from the source of life is destroyed. Through the 16, reunion with the great spirit is accomplished.

This can be a painful process, because it usually comes after much ego inflation. This results in a struggle between the ego and the divine will. Life presents challenges to your grand plans, which can be resented and struggled against. It is a lost battle, and you will likely feel humbled in the face of the collapse that follows. This humility is the key to later success, however, because you will learn to follow the intimations of a higher reality. In the destruction of the old, a spiritual rebirth takes place with an entirely new awareness. This rebirth affects every area of your life. It is a life much the better for the fall.

Those with the 16 Karmic Debt must be careful of egotism. Very often, those with the 16 use their highly intuitive and refined intellect to look down upon others, and view the rest of the world as inferior. This causes acute alienation and loneliness. In addition, it invites retribution, for the egotist is humbled more harshly than any other. When the 16 is in one of the core numbers, this process of destruction and rebirth is a continual cycle that actually serves to bring you into higher consciousness and closer union with the source of life.

The 16 Karmic Debt can be a path of progress and great spiritual growth if it is looked at properly. One develops great faith by placing one's life in the hands of God. Through such faith, gratitude and peace are firmly established.

KARMIC DEBT NUMBER 19

The person with the 19 Karmic Debt will learn independence and the proper use of power. You will be forced to stand up for yourself, and often be left to stand alone. Difficulties will be faced and overcome through personal struggle.

One of the central lessons for people with the 19 Karmic Debt is that you stubbornly resist help. Much of your independence is self-imposed; you simply don't want to listen to others, or to accept the help or advice of others. The 19 Karmic Debt can become a self-imposed prison if you do not open up to the reality of interdependence, and the mutual need for love.

The most important lesson for the 19 Karmic Debt is: While you seek to stand on your own feet, you are still a human being, deeply connected with others and in need of the support, assistance, and human understanding that all people need. Those with the 19 Karmic Debt will learn the hard way that "no man is an island," and that we are, indeed, "all bits of the main!"

Chapter 9: Being At The Right Place At The Right Time

Timing is everything for matters of luck.

So the cliché "Being at the right place at the right time" holds true.

You have to religiously observe the windows or cycles when you can usher in abundance or the winds of change.

The windows which will enhance your levels of success are:

1

3

6

8

These windows are your Personal Years or Personal Months or Personal Days in Numerology.

Take me, for instance. I was also born on the 28th. I bought my 4-room flat in the East during the property boom in 1996 (during a Personal Year 1) at $287,500. I managed to get an offer for it at $368,000 in 2010 (a Personal Year 6) before the cooling measures for the property market kicked in because I had a nagging feeling that the time was 'right' to let go of my property. It did not matter if I did not get the desired price, which was an optimistic $400,000. Soon after, the Housing and Development Board set in place measures to cool the speculators' market but thank goodness, I had made a pretty decent amount of profit. Before I discovered numerology, there were a few unsuccessful attempts at disposing my property but the timing just wasn't right. The property's address added up to number 8 and plagued me with money problems. Often, the electricity in my flat got disconnected because I could ill afford to pay the utility bills. On many occasions, my mother fell and fainted in the house, and I had to summon the ambulance. When I mastered the skill of numerology, I managed to unscramble the secret behind her birthdate. My mum's birth year was just recorded on her identity card; no day and month were visible. Rather bizarre. According to my sister, we have to use 1 January as her 'birthday' since no date was available. In that way, it was decoded that she is a number 8, a "Child of Fate" and the house being an 8, proved unlucky for her. It also drained my financial resources as she is my dependent and I had to foot all her medical bills. House number 8 made my mum really ill and made me wish I could just pack up and disappear from the face of this earth. That was a low point in my life. It was nothing like my teachers told me in school – work hard, get good grades and you will have a bright future! Despite the glowing testimonial that my school principal in junior college gave that stated I was "an above average student", I failed to fathom how I could attract ass luck because I worked my butt off during those difficult years.

After my house got sold, you cannot imagine the great relief and comfort I experienced when the burden of debt was lifted and I could waltz through life, foot loose! However that is not going to deter me from purchasing another piece of real estate and repeating sweet success. I must confess that I did experience a 2-week delay in receiving my check for the completion of sale as the resale officer's first name added up to 5 - the shadow side of this number denotes someone who may not deliver what he promises as he is irresponsible.

Now go fast forward and read the next chapter on lucky individuals who cashed in on the property craze. You will observe that some of them share the same cycles. If you embrace the same timings and golden numbers, you too, can cash in on the property market in good times.

In Chapter 5, you will be able to decode the meanings of Personal Years, Personal

Months and Personal Days in order for you to benefit from your windows of luck.

Chapter 10: Finding The Life Path Number

Your Life Path (or Destiny) Number is the most important of all your personal numbers. It reveals your purpose in life, the job you are here to do, and the path you must walk to do it. It deals with matters both spiritual and mundane, and in showing how those things are not only inter-related but indivisible, makes it clear why you have specific talents and abilities, and allows you to see and make sense of those assets in a new way.

The Life Path Number is found by adding the day, month, and year of birth and reducing it to a single digit – unless, of course, the calculation brings up one of the Master Numbers (11 or 22), which need not be reduced. For example 6th October 1947 would produce Life Path Number 1:

Day 6 = 6

Month 10 = 1 + 0 = 1

Year 1947 = 1 + 9 + 4 + 7 = 21, 2 + 1 = 3

6 + 1 + 3 = 10, 1 + 0 = 1

while 4th March 1930 would produce Life Path Number 11:

Day 4 = 4

Month 3 = 3

Year 1930 = 1 + 9 + 3 = 13, 1 + 3 = 4

4 + 3 + 4 = 11

Because the Life Path Number is so important, you will find both Keywords and explanatory text relating to each of the Primary and Master Numbers. However, as I pointed out in the previous Chapter, whilst preliminary notes can be constructed solely of Keywords, really comprehensive notes are invaluable when the job of final interpretation is staring you unavoidably in the face.

Totting up your own figures, finding your own Life Path Number, making the necessary notes (however good!), and hastening on to the next Chapter is not a very good idea either.

Whilst numbers certainly 'vibrate' differently according to the category in which they appear, their basic 'character' and meaning remains the same irrespective of category or placement, and much essential basic information about them can be learned from the information given in this Chapter. As some of those numbers will inevitably be relevant to your own Chart, it is worthwhile treating each Life Path Number as if it were your own – reading, thinking, and making hard copy notes that you can refer to as and when you need them.

You will find 'Ghost Notes' relating to Mary Jane Smith's Chart at the end of this Chapter. If you have decided to work with Mary Jane, try to answer the questions fully and add any further questions or ideas that occur to you to your own Notes.

MEANINGS OF LIFE PATH NUMBERS

Number 1 Life Path – Pioneer/Entrepreneur

Pros: Independence, adventure, initiative, originality, determination, individuality, direction.

Cons: Selfishness, intolerance, tyranny, laziness, indecision, resentfulness, officiousness.

This is a life path that offers every prospect of an interesting and successful life. One is the number of ruling, directing, inventing and planning, and Number 1 Life Path people are predominantly mental and introverted types. They are natural leaders, and need the freedom to be independent, make their own decisions, express their individuality and chart the course of their own lives. Ones not only have the ability to begin successful projects of their own; they are also capable of successfully completing projects begun by other people that might otherwise fail. They are determined and adventurous, and have excellent powers of concentration and the ability to overcome any obstacles to their success if they are allowed to follow and express their own creative ideas. However, they make good 'team workers' only if they are in charge of the team. Ones need to learn self-expression through unity and understanding, rather than through dominance and control. Danger lies in becoming egotistical, intolerant, over-confident, selfish and domineering when in a dominant position; being lazy, resentful, subversive and indecisive when not in a dominant position; and failing to listen to advice or admit a fault at any time.

Number 2 Life Path – Diplomat/Mediator

Pros: Diplomacy, mediation, adaptability, caution, kindness, sensitivity, co-operation, emotion, feeling, intuition.

Cons: Moodiness, imagining slights or wrongs, carrying grudges, self-deprecation, being overly tolerant, obsession with detail.

Two is the number of the heart rather than the mind and of service through healing. Number 2 Life Path people cannot live without others, and it is their tact and diplomacy, and their consideration for, and co-operation with, other people that usually bring them success and happiness. Twos tend to be cautious and methodical, and like to stick to working methods they know to be valid and functional. As they mature, they tend to prefer to visit or patronise places they know well and where they are known rather than trying somewhere or something completely new. Twos are very good at making contact and staying in touch with people; their warmth, sympathy, and understanding are attractive to others, and they tend to be generally well-liked and to have many acquaintances; friends, however, tend to be old friends. Number 2 Life Path people are intuitive, very sensitive to the feelings of others, very easily hurt themselves, sometimes naïve, and often shy. They need the praise and approbation of friends and colleagues, and are generous when judging or praising others. Danger lies in being too trusting, confiding in the wrong people, becoming over-emotional and moody, brooding over imaginary slights, or thinking poorly of the self and ones own achievements.

Number 3 Life Path – Individual/Self-Expression

Pros: Enthusiasm, inspiration, imagination, skill with words, vision, optimism, pleasure, creativity, ease, happiness, animation, artistic, cordiality.

Cons: Avarice, impatience, vanity, gossip, snobbishness, boasting, conceit, cynicism, cruelty in speech.

Three is the number of expression, declamation, and enunciation, and Number 3 Life Path people are usually offered the means of self-expression through speech or writing. Success – and the luxury and pleasant surroundings they enjoy – usually follows if they network, develop their contacts and associations, and work hard at honing their creative powers and use them to bring pleasure to others. Threes are clever, witty, and charming; they make entertaining companions, so people tend to seek them out and make them the focal point of any meeting, the centre of any group. Danger lies in failing to seize opportunities as they arise, entertaining a false self-image, becoming pessimistic and cynical when a single project fails or when success arrives too slowly, being hyper-critical of others, and impatient with or unkind to people less talented, intelligent or quick witted than they are themselves.

Number 4 Life Path – Practical/Organiser

Pros: Concentration, management, application, conservation, dedication, efficiency, organisation, follow-through.

Cons: Stubbornness, unreliability, weakness, carelessness, failure to concentrate, indulgence in fruitless argument and debate, use of violence to reach ends.

Four is a heavy, physical number, the number of analysis and discussion. Number 4 Life Path people are strong-willed, serious, tenacious, obstinate and determined, and often find a place in the military or some other similarly highly structured working environment. Routine, system, and detail are very important to them; they dislike change unless notified of it well in advance. Fours can find life very hard work – they often find themselves restricted by duty, their responsibility to others, or the need to economise – but this is a 'cornerstone number' and Fours usually find themselves rewarded for their work and endurance, albeit that those rewards tend to come slowly and always have to be earned. Success comes from being responsible, efficient, dutiful and hard working and building for the future – quite often a future that will be enjoyed by other people rather than themselves. Danger lies in using willpower destructively to rebel against almost everything, carelessness, unreliability, being too strict with family or fellow workers, indulging in fruitless argument and debate, or having recourse to violent behaviour in order to carry a point.

Number 5 Life Path – Communicator/Seeker of Experience & Change

Pros: Expansiveness, invention, promotion, variety, adventure, flexibility, movement, adjustment, change.

Cons: Promiscuity, deceitfulness, avoidance of responsibility, indebtedness, over-indulgence in food or alcohol, drug dependency.

Five is the number of display, duality and dexterity. Number 5 Life Path people are quick to think and act, generally brighter than average, love freedom, variety and change, and dislike routine or monotony. They generally choose careers related to travel, communication or sales, but may go through a number of jobs in a number of different areas before settling to a career. Number 5 is the number of sexual attraction and magnetism; Fives are usually strongly attracted, and very attractive to, the opposite sex. The 5 Life Path is all about movement, change, variety, travel, freedom, and constant adaptation to life's little ups and downs. The path is really about learning how to use freedom – which means learning to prepare for and accept and adapt to change but not to seek it - and understanding that freedom and permanence or security are often incompatible. Success comes through travel, learning foreign languages and different ways of living, keeping up with new technology and using it, and generally staying abreast of what's going on in the world. Danger lies in promiscuity or any kind of self-indulgence or foolish experimentation, deceitfulness, unreliability, using a natural facility with speech to fool or defraud other people, avoidance of responsibility, and carelessness about money.

Number 6 Life Path – Responsible/Practical

Pros: Beauty, sympathy, creativity, domesticity, healing, morality, passion, harmony, trust, service, musical talent.

Cons: Selfishness, jealousy, neediness in craving attention, affection or public appreciation of tasks undertaken, avoidance of responsibility.

Number 6 Life Path people are extrovert, sympathetic, attractive and loving, essentially practical, and conservative in their views and ideas. They have a strong desire for harmony, love, and a settled home-life and have a pronounced flair for beauty, colour and art. Sixes usually find people of difficult temperament in their immediate surroundings, and therefore need to learn to serve lovingly and cheerfully and to be an efficient and patient peace-maker. Sixes are likely to find themselves pushed into assuming responsibility for others, whether at work or at home, and are frequently people who are never much noticed (or, alas, truly appreciated!) until they are not there, when the absence of their quiet and harmonious input and willingness to help is very noticeable indeed, but success can bring financial rewards, as well as the affection and admiration of other people. Danger lies in adopting a narrow exclusive attitude to loved ones, friends and possessions, jealousy, making frequent complaints that lead to quarrels, avoiding responsibility or refusing to accept it, or taking on too much responsibility, thus making other people too dependant.

Number 7 Life Path– Mental Analysis/Wisdom

Pros: Analysis, research, calculation, understanding, perfection, the unseen, intuition, investigation, reason, vision, solitude, creative, artistic, retirement, reserve.

Cons: Spiritual pride, using knowledge gained to build a 'cult of personality, escapism, refusal to face reality, fear of loneliness or failure.

Seven is the number of the stoic and the mystic, and the Number 7 Life Path is the path of inspirational spiritual insight. Seven Life Path people tend to be self-sufficient introverts, thinkers, mystics, philosophers and loners whose task it is to look for the truths that underlie the appearance of things, and so attain wisdom. Sevens tend to be silent, aloof, selective and solitary people attracted to things secret, mysterious, or ancient. They really need peace and quiet; in fact it is essential that Sevens learn to be alone and like it, because for them all answers must come from within, and can be sought and found only in silence and solitude. Sevens can be markedly creative and artistic, but they do not fit easily into the modern world; success comes when they can escape the hustle and bustle of too much noise and too many people, and confine their construction of theories and search for meaning to a single area. Danger lies in spiritual pride, building a cult of personality, desire to escape from reality, refusal to face self and problems as they really are, overindulgence in drugs or alcohol, and fearing loneliness or failure.

Number 8 Life Path – Financier/Commercial Power

Pros: Power, authority, capability, organisation, efficiency, skill, hard work.

Cons: Materialism, avarice, greed.

Eight is the number of material achievement, self-assertiveness and business success. Number 8 Life Path people are energetic, ambitious, capable realists - poised, assured, and self-controlled. Eights are discriminating, authoritative and materialistic. They are prepared to work relentlessly toward their goals, and are often attracted to the commercial or financial world or to the 'corridors of power' – politics and the civil service. Eight is a power number, and the Number 8 Life Path is that of material values, material freedom, practical financial ideas, organisation and success. Nevertheless, in order to truly succeed, Eights must be prepared to have other than purely material values, and work hard and constructively for the good of the community as a whole. Eights are not cold people (in fact they are more emotionally dependant on others than they like to admit) but often find it difficult to express their feelings. Money and security are usually taken very seriously into account when it comes to marriage or partnerships of any kind. Danger lies in avarice and greed, driving the self or other people too hard, and forgetting that life has a spiritual side.

Number 9 Life Path – Universal Love/Service

Pros: Creativity, imagination, benevolence, intuition, philanthropy, emotion, generosity, devotion, dedication.

Cons: Selfishness, narrow-mindedness, impersonality, busy-body.

The Number 9 Life Path is the path of service to the world community, and Nines are strong characters, independent, self-assured, energetic, optimistic, generous and compassionate. Nines tend to seek out opportunities that allow them a broad scope of usefulness – religious ministry, foreign fields of service and enterprise, philanthropic or charitable organisations - where their sense of adventure and need to serve bring them happiness and fulfilment. Success comes through cultivating a wide-vision, broadminded, interested-in-everything attitude to life and taking part in broad-scope projects – humanitarian schemes, charities, national or international movements – where attention to detail and willingness to see things through to completion are essential. Danger lies in prejudiced, narrow-minded or intolerant thinking and attitudes. Nines – in their sincere anxiety to help others, right wrongs, and make the world a better place – often find it a trial to avoid these failings, and difficult to understand that 'good' as they see it may not be suitable to specific places and/or people.

Number 11 Life Path – Intuition/Teaching & Idealism

Pros: Aware, psychic, creative, discerning, dreamy, inspiring, intense, inventive, progressive.

Cons: Eccentric, worrying.

Eleven is a Master Number, and people who have this Life Path and chose to follow it have strong spiritual insight, are idealistic and visionary, inventive, progressive and intuitive, and are frequently unconventional and unorthodox in their beliefs. Attracted to the mystical and the occult, they are often neither readily accepted nor easily understood by other people, and usually meet with opposition in many guises as they make their way through life. Success comes through developing a philosophical attitude to life and making sure that inventive ideas are guided into practical channels. Danger lies in becoming an eccentric, a crank, or an impractical dreamer, and worrying too much about things that can't be changed.

This number can be reduced to two, and all of the characteristics of that number underlie this one. If your Life Path is Eleven, you should therefore read about it in conjunction with Life Path Number 2.

Number 22 Life Path – Builder/Idealist

Pros: Achievement, wisdom, ingenuity, energy, innovation, perfectionism and idealism.

Cons: Destructive, dramatic, over-emotional.

Twenty-two is the number of great achievement, and the Number 22 Life Path is often associated with healing organisations, spiritual foundations, charities and social welfare schemes. Twenty-twos have the ability to unite practical skills with high ideals and imaginative and constructive ideas, but their intensity and perfectionism can be difficult for other people to deal with. Twenty-two is a Master Number, and people who have this Life Path Number and choose to follow it are 'broad-stroke' people who need to allow others to work out the nitty-gritty details of the projects they envisage. Success comes when they can hold on to the vision of their ideas as a whole; danger lies in worrying over details, or getting side-tracked by other people who worry too much about details.

Twenty-two can be reduced to Four, and all the characteristics of that number underlie this one. If your Life Path Number is 22, you should therefore read about it in conjunction with Life Path Number 4.

Master Numbers – To Reduce or Not To Reduce?

People tend to talk about reducing Master Numbers as though this were just a matter of making a deliberate decision, like turning left or right at the crossroads or opting for black shoes rather than brown ones, but of course it isn't like that at all. I have an Eleven Life Path, and I find that I naturally oscillate between one vibration and the other in response to circumstances. I think it likely that all Elevens and Twenty-twos oscillate in the same way – and that more often than not they spend most of their lives behaving like regular Twos and Fours – so I always take both numbers into account equally when Master Numbers turn up in a Chart.

Chapter 11: The Hierophant

The Hierophant card is also known as the Teacher card. The early card has undergone some significant changes during the period of the Dark Age. I prefer to give it a more secular interpretation. The teacher is a well learnt person and a master of sacred customs. Disciples kneel before him and listen to his wisdom; the robes of the disciples bear a design of red roses and white lilies which symbolize desire and abstract thought respectively. People who fall under the influence of this vibration are natural leaders and are destined to share some unique expertise or experience with others. These people may acquire wisdom through another mentor or through their personal experiences. They are orthodox and sometimes stubborn and exasperating. They assume the role of guardians of traditions, religious knowledge or may even come up with their own philosophy of religion and God. However these great teachers should be open to new ideas and encourage their followers to formulate or draw their own conclusions. Taurus the Earthly bull is the sign of a holy man. This makes them reluctant to make any changes in their life. But on the positive side, they strive to create harmony and peace in the midst of a crisis. At their best, they are wise and soothing, at their worst, they are unbending traditionalists. They are also concerned with outward appearances and like to impress others. In the lower octave, these teachers or preachers should not be rigid or forcible in rubbing their doctrines on others.

Rabindranath Tagore

Key Compound Number 5

Rabindranath Tagore was a Bengali polymath who reshaped his region's literature and music. He became the first non-European Nobel laureate by earning a Prize in Literature for "Gitanjali". His poetry was viewed as spiritual and mercurial. His seemingly mesmeric persona, floccose locks, and empyreal garb garnered him a prophet-like aura in the West. As a humanist, Universalist and strident anti-nationalist he denounced the British government and advocated for independence from Britain. As an exponent of the Bengal Renaissance, he advanced a vast canon that comprised paintings, sketches and doodles, hundreds of texts, and some two thousand songs. Tagore's legacy endures also in the institution he founded, Visva-Bharati University where classes are conducted under trees and close to nature. This esteemed university produced several prominent personalities in diversified spheres like Supreme Court judges, entrepreneurs and a Nobel laureate. Tagore penned two national anthems: the Republic of India's Jana Gana Mana and Bangladesh's Amar Shonar Bangla. Gandhi is often referred to as Mahatma meaning "Great Soul," an honorific first applied to him by Rabindranath Tagore.

THE LOVERS

Originally, this card was called just 'Love'. And that's actually more apt than

"Lovers". The two figures in the Lovers card are blessed and protected by the infinite intelligence in the clouds above them. The sign associated with the Lovers is Gemini that is ruled by mercury, the planet of communication. Just like the sunshine, transparent communication and trust brings warmth and security to a healthy relationship. The twelve flames in the picture, signifies that the twelve zodiac signs are no exception to the grace of love. Love is a force that makes you choose and decide for reasons you often cannot understand; it makes you surrender control to a higher power. This could be a person, place or a thing. Love is usually followed by the feeling of compassion.

People who fall under the influence of this number are very sensitive and make good spouses, parents and home makers. They are very social and cannot live without the society. These people love to take responsibility of their beloved ones. Usually they do not stick to anything for long be it a job, cause, venture or a person. These courageous, original and brilliant natives have the potential to become great reformers or catalysts for change in home, work and or society provided these people stick to their guns. Beauty in all forms is well appreciated and career in aesthetics, like cosmetics, jeweler and interior designing, arts, poetry and literature will also satiate their soul's passion. On the lower octave, infidelity, irresponsible behavior and over indulgence in the aesthetics of life will

Sigmund Freud

Name Number 6

Sigmund Freud was a Jewish Austrian neurologist who founded the psychoanalytic school of psychiatry. Freud is best known for his theories of the unconscious mind and the defense mechanism of repression. The most significant contribution Freud made to Western thought were his arguments concerning the importance of the unconscious mind in understanding conscious thought and behavior. Freud called dreams the "royal road to the unconscious". This meant that dreams illustrate the "logic" of the unconscious mind. He theorized that personality is developed by a person's childhood experiences. On the lower octave of number six, Freud was addicted to smoking. A heavy cigar smoker, Freud smoked 20 cigars a day despite health warnings from colleagues. Freud was eventually diagnosed with an oral cancer. Despite over 30 surgeries, and complications ranging from intense pain to insects infesting dead skin cells around the cancer, Freud smoked cigars until his life ended in a morphine-induced coma to relieve the pain. In September 1939, he prevailed on his doctor and friend Max Schur to assist him in suicide. After taking permission from Freud's wife, Schur administered three doses of morphine over many hours that resulted in Freud's death.

THE CHARIOT

The Chariot is one of the most majestic cards in the set of 22 Major Arcana. A royal prince rides in a chariot drawn by two horses, black and white representing mercy and severity respectively. The prince keeps both of them in line with a wand of willpower, for if he doesn't the horses will pull him in opposite directions leading to disaster. The Chariot card is not about riding majestically through the town. It is the victory which creates kingship as its natural consequence and not the vested royalty of the fourth card 'Emperor'. This card promises triumph and victory through self-mastery, and the bringing together of powerful and possibly conflicting forces to work in harmony towards a common goal. Those who fall under the influence of this number are assured of victory if they overcome their doubts and fear, and work towards their goal with continued effort. Honor, fame, recognition, awards and monetary rewards will eventually follow their success. These people should exercise discipline and harness their inner strength and use it wisely. Wasted energy is wasted effort. This card also suggests long distance travel, experimentation and/or exploration.

George Washington

Name Number 88 Key Compound Number

George Washington was a dominant military and political leader of USA who led the American victory over Great Britain in the American Revolutionary War as commander-in-chief of the continental army. Historians give Washington high marks for his selection and supervision of his generals; encouragement of morale and ability to hold together the army; coordination with the state governors and state militia units; relations with Congress; and attention to supplies, logistics, and training. In his domestic life, he managed a variety of enterprises. He freed all the slaves in his tobacco plantation. After victory, he drafted the US Constitution and was elected as the first President of USA. Washington had a vision of a great and powerful nation that would be built on republican lines using federal power. He sought to use the national government to preserve liberty, improve infrastructure, open the western lands, promote commerce, found a permanent capital, reduce regional tensions and promote a spirit of American nationalism. Washington presided over the creation of a strong, well-financed national government that stayed neutral in the wars raging in Europe, suppressed rebellion and won acceptance among Americans of all types. His leadership style established many forms and rituals of government that have been used since, such as using a cabinet system and delivering an inaugural address. Washington is universally regarded as the

"Father of his Country".

STRENGTH

The card is illustrated by a woman in white dress taming a wild lion on a rugged landscape. White color symbolizes peace and purity of thought. She also wears a crown and a robe made of red roses. Red rose symbolizes love, passion and desire.

The infinite symbol signifies that the woman's inner strength is infinite. There is no evidence of power struggle, yet the woman controls the wild lion with sheer will power. That is exactly what Eight's do. People under the influence of this number make excellent entrepreneurs. They work hard to achieve their goals and possess a special skill of making money in leaps and bounds. However they should avoid being impulsive, critical and stubborn. Usually these people have a tendency to ill treat or get frustrated with those who do not meet their expectations. These people form strong opinions and become too judgmental. Eights do not always have a smooth ride in their endeavors just like the rugged field beneath in the picture. Yet, these people overcome all obstacles with courage and enthusiasm.

John D. Rockefeller

Key Compound Number 8

John D. Rockefeller was an American oil magnate. He revolutionized the petroleum industry and defined the structure of modern philanthropy. He founded the Standard Oil Company and aggressively ran it until his retirement. As kerosene and gasoline grew in importance, Rockefeller's wealth soared, and he became the world's richest man and first American worth more than a billion dollars. Adjusting for inflation, he is often regarded as the richest and controversial businessman in history. From his very first pay check, Rockefeller tithed ten percent of his earnings to his church. As his wealth grew, so did his giving, primarily to educational and public health causes, but also for basic science and the arts. His fortune was mainly used to create the modern systematic approach of targeted philanthropy with foundations that had a major effect on medicine, education, and scientific research. Rockefeller University, founded by Rockefeller claims a connection to 23 Nobel laureates so far. Rockefeller adhered to total abstinence from alcohol and tobacco throughout his life. He spent the last 40 years of his life in retirement.

THE HERMIT

The card is depicted by a Sage standing alone on a snowy peak, lighting the way for others with the Lamp of Truth or Light of the World in the lantern that he holds.

There is a great difference between loneliness and aloneness. When there is no "significant other" in our lives we can either be lonely, or enjoy the freedom that solitude brings. When we find no support among others for our deeply felt truths, we can either feel isolated and bitter, or celebrate the fact that our vision is strong enough even to survive the powerful human need for the approval of family, friends or colleagues. The long grey beard of the Hermit implies ages of wisdom acquired through past experiences. The humble figure in this card glows with a light that emanates from within. One of Gautama Buddha's most significant contributions to the spiritual life of humankind was to insist to his disciples, "Be a light unto you". Ultimately, each of us must develop within ourselves the capacity to make our way through the darkness without any companions, maps or guide. Hence, it is a card of attainment of the spiritual wisdom and the sage stands vigil for weary seekers willing to share it. The snow represents the isolation he endures because his wisdom sets him apart from others.

Those under the influence of this vibration are humanitarians born for the service of others. These people have a thirst for spiritual knowledge and an urge for freedom and wisdom that transcends personal needs. The higher they evolve the more difficulties they face. People will be drawn to them for advice. Charitable work is close to their heart. These people easily acquire money and independence.

Mikhail Gorbachev

Key Compound Number 9

Mikhail Gorbachev is a former Soviet statesman, and the last head of state of the USSR. Gorbachev's attempts at reform as well as summit conferences with United States President Ronald Reagan and his reorientation of Soviet strategic aims contributed to the end of the Cold War and also ended the political supremacy of the Communist Party, and led to the dissolution of the Soviet Union. For these efforts, he was awarded the Nobel Peace Prize.

Chapter 12: Your Lucky Numbers

This is the interesting part of the whole exercise. You already know your most important - and therefore, luckiest - numbers, and you also know the best days to use them. Unfortunately, for most purposes you need longer numbers than simply one or two digits. If you just need a single number-say for instance that the horse-use your most important numbers in descending order, and try and place the bet on the right day for you

However, say you require a six -digit number, or maybe a series of two digit numbers for Lotto. All you do is create a number which when brought down to a single digit, equates to your most important numbers.

Let's use John Connolly again. His most important numbers are (in order) 5, 6, 8 and 9. Assume he wants a six-digit number to buy a lottery ticket. His best course is to buy a lottery ticket with a number on it that reduces to one of his numbers. If he had a choice of 764356, 764357, 764358 from one book, and 29466, 29467 and 29470 from another, which ticket should he choose? His fIrst choice should be 764357 as that reduces to 5, but he might also decide to buy 764358 (which reduces to a 6) or 29466 (which reduces to a 9). If he could afford to buy just one ticket, he should choose the one that adds up to his Most Important number. To try and put every advantage his way, he should also buy the ticket on the right day as well.

With Lotto numbers you have to work out the numbers yourself. This is also a simple matter. Good numbers for John would be 5, 14, 23 and 32 as they all reduce to his Most Important Number. He could add to this 6, 15, 24 and 33 (which reduce to 6), 8, 17, 26 and 35 (which reduce to 8. Isn't he lucky having an 8 in his name!), and also 9, 18, 27, and 36 (which reduce to 9).

These numbers are likely to prove effective particularly if John uses them at the right time. Want more numbers? No problem. Simply add your Most Important Numbers to your Personal Day number. In John's case, again using March 25th, 1988, we know he is in a 3 Personal Day. If we add 3 to each of his main numbers (5,6,8 and 9) we end up with 8 (!), 9, 11 and 3 (1+2=3). We have already used the 8 and the 9 in John's case, but we can create anew set of numbers out of the 11 and 3.2, 11,20 and 33 from the 11, and 3, 12,21, and 30 from the 3.

This example shows one major exception to the general rule. On March 25th, 1988 John should use the number 8 in preference to his most Important Number, as it crops up twice - once as one of his main numbers, and again when it is added to his Personal Day number. This is an exceptionally strong money combination, so he should definitely capitalize on it as much as possible.

YOUR CURRENT NAME

It is possible that you are no longer using the name you were born with. For instance, you may have changed it through marriage, altered the spelling of it, dropped one of the names - or even changed it entirely. If this is the case, you should work out the numbers of your current name and you can use these in the same way as the main numbers. Remember that the numbers from the name you were given at birth remain the most important no matter how many times you change your name. People who believe in reincarnation say that we actually choose our own names before we are born to get the experiences we need in this lifetime.

Let's take our friend John Horatio Connolly as an example again. As we already know, his main numbers are 5, 6, 8 and 9. Suppose, that as a child, all his friends called him 'Jack' and the name somehow stuck. He was always embarrassed with the name 'Horatio', so dropped it entirely once he grew up. So he is now known to everyone as 'Jack Connolly'.

1 6 6 7 =20=2 JACK CONNOIL Y 1 32 3 55 33 =25=7

Using this name Jack Connolly gains an Expression number of 9 and a Soul Urge number of 2 (the second and third most important numbers). He already has a 9 in his original main numbers, but he can utilize the 2 in working out lucky numbers for himself.

In fact, if he is usually known as 'Jack', rather than 'Jack Connolly', he could also use the 7 and I from that name. However, he should only do this if he is wanting new numbers all the time, rather than repeating previously used ones. In this instance he would add them to his Personal Day number and use them on that particular day. "

Using this name Jack Connolly Gains an Expression number of 9 and a Soul Urge number of 2 (the second and third most important numbers). He already has a 9 in his original main numbers, but he can utilize the 2 in working out lucky numbers for himself.

In fact, if he is usually known as "Jack", rather than "John Connolly" you could also use the 7 and 1 from that name. However, you should only do this if he is wanting new numbers all the time, rather than repeating previously used ones. In this instance he would add them to his Personal Day number and use them on that particular day.

YOUR SUCCESS NUMBER

This number is not always a 'lucky number', but can bring benefits if you can make your signature total this number. It is extremely easy to work out your personal success number.

If you were born on a 1, 5 or 7 day your success number is 5. These days are the 1 st, 5th, 7th, 10th, 14th, 16th, 19th, 23rd, 25th or 28th of any month.

If you were born on a 2, 4 or 8 day your success number is 8. These days are the 2nd, 4th, 8th, lith, 13th, 17th, 20th, 22nd, 26th, 29th or 31 st of any month.

If you were born on a 3,6 or 9 day your success number is 6. These days are the 3,6,9,12,15,18,21,24,27,or 30 of any month.

Let's look at John Connolly again. As he was born on the 9th day of the month (9th December, 1946) his signature should total 6. Interestingly enough, his entire name does already add up to 6, so he could be very successful signing his entire name as his signature. However, he has never liked the name 'Horatio', so does not wish to sign his name with the hated middle name in it. We'll experiment with a few possibilities.

667 =19=1. J.H. CONNOLLy 18 355 33 =28=1

This name totals 2, so is not likely to be as successful for him as using his full name. Here's another possibility:

6 6 6 7 =25=7 JOHN H. CONNOLL Y

185835533 =41=5

This totals 3 (12, and 1 +2=3), so it would be a good name for someone who wanted to be well liked. (3 = sociability, creativity, getting on with others, self-expression). However, it still doesn't give us the 6 he should have to be successful.

6 6 6 7 =25=7 JOHN CONNOLL Y 1853 5533 =33=6

This signature is likely to be the least successful as it totals a 4 (hard work, drudgery, slow and steady progress).

Even using his present name, Jack Connolly, we do not get a total of 6. It looks as if he will have to change the spelling of the name 'John' or insert a fictitious initial to make the signature total6.

Isn't it wrong to use an initial that doesn't mean anything? Certainly not if it makes your path through life that little bit easier. There are any number of historical precedents. Even Pythagoras, the father of modem Numerology, experimented with many different names to experience the vibrations associated with each number. It also does not have to be simply an initial. You may have a favorite name that, when added to your usual signature creates a total equal to your Success Number. If so, use it. If it is important to you that the initial means something, try using the initial of your mother's maiden name, or perhaps the initial of a close friend or someone you have always admired.

To get back to Mr. Connolly again, he could decide to use John H C. Connolly or John T. Connolly if he wanted to add an initial. Naturally, the sky is the limit if you wanted to add an entire new middle name.

Another important aspect to your signature is that it should be legible. In graphology, an indecipherable signature denotes someone who has something to hide. Unless that is the image you wish to convey, practice on creating a legible signature.

Chapter 13: Ragu - Uranus (Number- 4)

People who are born under the days 4,13,22 or 31 or the date total by adding all the digits of the date to single number which becomes 4 or as per numerology if the name total gives sum with the number 4 (like 4,13,22,31,40,49,etc) are coming under Ragu/ Uranus power.

Number 4 indicates Ragu/ Uranus and it reforms the people. These people speak interestingly and they like travelling. They learn important things accurately so that they can explain them to others. Lord Ganesa is the deity of this number. People with this number can reform the world with their speech and writing.

They speak truth boldly and they will have an overall idea about anything. They don't have many friends. These people are attracted towards stories, scriptures, Philosophy and religious texts. The important character of these people is that they want to know everything.

Even the smallest harsh words will hurt them. They will quickly get heart-broken. They are too sensitive. These people will indulge in works where they can win without difficulties.

After 40 years these people may become anaemic and it is better to take foods that will increase digestive power.

People born under 4: They are strict, strong and courageous. They should restrict themselves in food and sensory pleasures. They need to be calm when unexpected incidents take place. They must try to speak sweetly and attractively.

People born under 13: Shocking things happen in their life unexpectedly. Dangers come and go. Changes in the family will affect their childhood. These strong people must be honest and truthful in order to lead a good life. They will face lot of problems because of women.

People born under 22: Evil attracts them rather than goodness. They will get ample opportunities to get into evil path. Good administrators who earns money easily. They are surrounded by people who can deceive them. They earn money through competitions betting and through evil deeds. It is important to have Noble one's friendship.

People born under 31: People born under this number are courageous and are mentally strong. Even new ones can find out within few minutes that these people are not ordinary people. They can defeat their enemies however they are. They like to be in solitude and they indulge in philosophy. They need to restrict themselves from sensory pleasures.

So, check the numbers and alphabets in the introduction chapter and find your name digits or sum accordingly. If not lucky, change letters or names to good numbers as said above.

Names and number 4:

You will be ruled by RAGU/ URANUS or the number 4 if you have the name total as 4 by adding up all the alphabets numbers making a single digit. (**RAJ** = 2+1+1=4) But, remember that the people born under 4 (Either the date or sum of date digits) mostly can have names under 4. Also anyone with lucky numbers under 4 can have their names which will not harm them. Then only it will give good results. Mostly avoid names under 4.

Good and Bad Numbers Under 4 (for names by adding all the alphabets' digits)
4- There won't be luck in accordance to fame. Unwanted fears prevail. They will have diseases and opposition. Knowing everything they need to live how others tell them to be.

13- Foreigners are afraid of this number. Lord Rama is the perfect example for this number.

Though he didn't want to punish others he did. People with this number will face unexpected bad things and they will face difficulties because of ladies. Though their status becomes high they will always be in a worry.

22- This number kindles senses. They are attracted to competition, betting, alcohol, sensory pleasures or any one of the thing. They gamble without fear and they may go to a situation where they might lose everything. Good administrators who can survive from any difficulties. They will get a bad fame.

31- They are concerned with freedom not profit and loss and they act as they wish though it is good or bad. Have involvement in mind-reading, astrology and philosophy. They live like a philosopher. Success doesn't give them its happiness. In the age of 31 they may liberate everything or lose them. In 37 it will be reverted. They will face an unexpected ending.

40- People with this number get unexpected friendship through which they attain higher status and commanding jobs. Gain fame, money and jewels. Evil traits get exposed. They can achieve anything. But in the end life will be useless. They will say that society dint accept their service and they will lose all their wealth. Their end will be very bad.

49- People with this number will be wealthy, will do astonishing things and their fame spread like fire. There will be lot of travel. Rare experience takes place. Luck plays a good role. Unexpected accidents take place.

58- People with this number will be successful and their life will upgrade faster. They will be concerned with cleanliness, reformation and religion. If the birth date is 4 or 8 they will gain name and fame. People with this number will have some fear but they will feel lucky. If people born under different date get this number in name then the life which upgrade will degrade and will lead a selfish life with lot of difficulties.

67- These people are good artist and hard-working. Imagination, love and purity will make them as a nobleman. Have the support of people in higher post. They should be aware of imaginary women. Selfish deeds are ineffective. This number works only for artists.

76- People with this number may lose everything suddenly. They will be famous. They will be successful in social works. Gain wealth through astonishing sources. They will spend their old age simply by eating and sleeping.

85- This number indicates Hard-working people who defeat evil and wins. They will also solve others' problems. They will find new information related to religion and nature. They are efficient in Medical profession.

94- People with this number give good benefits to the world. They do general reforms.

Good life and fame will occur and revert. This number is a lucky number **103**- This is a lucky number. People with this number will gain wealth initially. Then there will be change in the job. Competitions occur. Life's end will be happy.

Lucky Days: 1,10,19,28 are good (Either day or sum of the digits in date). Days under 9, 18

and 27 will also help.

Important Days: 4, 13, 22 and 31. Good luck will work out automatically. Don't start any new task these days.

Unlucky Days: 8, 17 and 26. Avoid all the good start-ups or do not start anything in life in these days.

Work/Business: People with number 4 will be lecturers, novelist, artist, philosophical researcher, doctor, astrologer, singer, dancer, journal publisher, sales man. They might also involve in cow and horse trade, book publishing wood works, bus, lorry and cycle trade.

They might also organize competition and betting.

Marriage/Life partner: People under 4 may choose 1, 8, 4 or 6. They can also choose 7.

Lucky Colours: White, Blue and Yellow.

Lucky Stone: Hessonite (Gomedhagam) & Light Blue Stone.

Personalities under 4:

MARGARET THATCHER – 13-10-1925 – (4 & 4)

MICHAEL FARADAY – 22-09-1791 – (4 & 4)

Chapter 14: Recurring Number

Have you noticed certain numbers that keep recurring in your life? For example, you might notice that the number 4 keeps appearing from nowhere. If so, it might mean that you should focus on working for stability.

It is believed that the universe speaks to everyone. However, it does not communicate in a way that people usually do. Usually, the universe communicates using omens, signs, and symbols, and more importantly, using numbers. Therefore, if you notice a certain number keeps appearing in your life, then you should pause for a moment and reflect on it.

How the universe communicates through numbers

The universe gets its message across by showing you a certain number. With a strong willingness to connect and make you understand its message, the number may not stop recurring in your life until you understand its message or as long as you need such message to be understood. The number that will appear to you will vary depending on the message that the universe wants you to understand. Unfortunately, many people do not pay attention to these things and have no knowledge about the meaning of every number. However, if only you can stop for a moment and learn to be open to everything that is around you, you will know with certainty that, indeed, the universe is trying to communicate with you.

Be open

The most important step to be able to identify a recurring number (or numbers) is to be open. To be open means to have a willingness to listen to what the universe wants to tell you. An important part of being open is being conscious. Unfortunately, given today's hustle and bustle of daily life, most people act like robots that they are, in a way, unconscious of what they are doing.

Since a recurring number will appear several times, you would be able to identify it simply by being open. For example, perhaps you suddenly woke up at 4 am, received four calls in the morning, and noticed the number 4 several times while you were on your way to work. Take note that you do not have to see the number in writing, and indirect manifestation of it is enough. Also, it is possible that the universe is sending you more than a single number, especially when it wants you to work on more than a single facet of your life.

It is not always a problem

This is something that should be made clear. Not all recurring numbers mean something negative or come in the form of a warning. Unfortunately, most books on numerology always interpret a recurring number from a negative perspective. Sometimes, it can even be scary because it seems like you will face a terrible future if you fail to act upon the recurring number. So, to be clear, the message behind a recurring number can be a mere confirmation of something that is completely positive. For example, you have just become a leader of a group. Suddenly, you notice that the number 1 seems to be a recurring number. Does this mean that your leadership is being threatened and that you need to exert more effort into being a leader? No, most probably not. Instead, it may even mean that the universe is simply sending you a motivation, a reminder that you are a leader, but without any threat to your leadership. Of course, there is no one way of interpreting such message. To better understand what the universe is trying to tell you, you need to take a look at the circumstances and understand yourself.

Introspection

This is, by far, one of the most important things that you need, especially in understanding the true message of a recurring number. Introspection is also a basic practice in many esoteric systems. So, what is introspection?

Introspection simply means to understand one's self. You need to stop, be still, and know yourself. Accept your strengths and your weaknesses– especially your weaknesses. Look at your life as a mere spectator and try to better understand yourself. How is your spirituality? Also, how are your career and your relationship with your loved ones? By understanding who you are and where you really stand in life will help you understand the main point which a recurring is trying to tell you.

The message

There are three things that you should do when you notice a recurring number:

Know the qualities, traits, and properties of the recurring number.

Know what it is trying to tell you.

Take action.

For example, if you are about to embark on an exciting career but feel hesitant because of the new challenges that you will face and then, suddenly, you notice that the number 5 becomes a recurring number, then most probably, the universe is telling you to go ahead and grab the opportunity and face the challenges. Now, it is up to you to take action. Here is another example. You are getting fond of a particular person. You then notice that the numbers 6 and 9 have become recurring numbers. The combination of such recurring numbers may mean that the said person is a good match for you.

Although a number signifies different things, you may know exactly what a recurring number is trying to tell you if you engage in introspection. After all, a recurring number is telling you something about your life. By the simple process of deduction (removing those that do not apply to your life), you will easily know the quality or trait of a recurring number that applies to you.

Also, take note that numbers will not tell you to do something evil. For example, if you plan on killing someone, then suddenly notice that the number 1 becomes a recurring number. This does not mean that you should pursue on committing the crime. In fact, it most probably means that you should abandon your evil plan, and simply start a new life– a life without hatred and a life of love, harmony, and peace where you can be truly happy.

Chapter 15: The Philosophy Of Numbers

In all ancient teachings, references to numbers are frequent. Proof can be found in the Indian Vedas, Chinese books, including those of Confucius, the Hebrew Kabbalah compiled by the Jewish Rabbis, and the Egyptian rituals of the dead in Egyptian hieroglyphics that date back to 3,100 BC. Hebrew priests spread numerology to the Chaldeans, Phoenicians and the Chinese.

The ancient people, together with the Chaldeans and Egyptians, were masters of the occult or hidden meaning of numbers in their application and in their relation to human lives.

Philosophers of ancient Greece believed that numbers possessed mysterious powers. Pythagoreans believed that all things are assimilated to numbers.

Therefore, Pythagoras, in his sacred discourse, clearly stated: "Numbers are the rulers of forms and ideas and are the cause of Gods and demons."

Ptolemy, the great astrologer and numerologist of ancient Egypt, said, "Judgement must be regulated by yourself as well as by the science — it is advantageous to make choices of the days and hours at a time constituted by your birthday."

One essential prerequisite when calculating predictions or predicting one's future is that we should be more rational and philosophical. At the time of calculations, we should not be emotional or have preconceived notions. This particularly comes into play when we are calculating for our kith and kin or close friends or when someone is seriously ill or if someone is approaching us in a highly depressed or desperate mood.

Basically, we must remember that all the numbers can be lucky as well as unlucky. For example, a person who is very lucky, but has a wrong outlook on life or leads a life with nefarious intentions, will necessarily pay a heavy price and, therefore, may not find the numbers lucky. By the same token, an ordinary person with bad numbers still leads a humble and ordinary life with contentment. Because, as the Vedas say, no one can be totally lucky or unlucky from birth until death. This is because happiness is only a state of mind and how we look at life and lead our lives. As a great philosopher said,

"It is not worth understanding life but to live it, since no one gets out alive."

In spite of all this, everyone is curious at every stage of life as to what the future is holding for him or her. In this, numerology is most useful. Also, whether we are doctors, judges, students or housewives, all of us face many times in our lives when there are dual opportunities to take or choices to make. Here too, numerology can give a meaningful and useful direction.

Very often, all of us experience times of lost opportunities, failures or utter despondency. At this juncture, we all look for an answer as to why has this happened to me? Even in such dire situations, numerology helps by revealing why this period is bad and nothing could have been expected to happen. This provides a period of sobriety so that the person can meaningfully and philosophically analyse the events and thereby maintain tranquillity.

Remember, we are responsible for our actions alone; the net result is not in our hands. As is said, "You cannot argue your case and pass judgement too."

Chapter 16: Career Orientation

In the Galaxy of careers, we are often dazzled and confused which one we should opt for. Wrong selection of career might cause repentance, frustration and lack of job contentment. So, we ought to be very careful in career orientation.

Career orientation is a burning issue for most of us. We often think that what particular career we will like to adopt in life in which career we can better establish ourselves. Many a times, we are not able to become what we aspire for, in spite of all the aptitude n ability for a particular profession, because we are destined for some other career in life. At times, due to insistence of parents, we are not able to opt for subjects that we intend to study; sometimes financial imitations hinder attainment of our career targets. Health issues too, sometimes play a decisive role in career selection. Conclusively, we attain a career in life either based on our aptitudes, potentials or as destined my luck for us. Birth number and luck number both play vital role.

CAREER ORIENTATION TIPS

NUMBER 1

Most suitable professions for them are administrative services, management services, business executives, consultancy and leadership, miners of clay, dealers of white colored objects and dairy products.

Many great political leaders, administrators and religious heads are born under this number.

NUMBER 2

Most suitable professions are literary activity based jobs, artist, poet, translator, tourist guide, fashion designer, tourism related jobs, air services, aviation engineering & research and can be dealer of white, silver and grey colored objects, art wares and handicrafts.

NUMBER 3

Professions most suitable for them are education, study of literature and languages, running educational institutions, management, legal profession, hotel management, army, administrative services, home-management, architect, writer, event-manager, surgeon, occult studies, social activity and dealer of iron, gold, silver and property.

NUMBER 4

Business executive, event manager, leader, politician, social worker, scientist, banker, accountant, consultant, analyst, art gallery manager, designer, successful dealer in silver, white and grey colored objects, dairy products, handicrafts and antiques.

NUMBER 5

Psychiatrist, pediatrician, physiotherapist, music composer, choreographer, event manager, kindergarten teacher, exporter, banker, chartered accountant, business executive, foreign administrative services, sports correspondent, sportsman, reiki trainer, dealer of silver, sports material, music albums, utility items for children, white, grey and silvery objects.

NUMBER 6

Interior decorator, exhibitionist, curator, designer, architect, interior decorator, event management of fashion shows, film director, stock and share investors, art director, art critics, artists, curator, sexologist, beautician, dealer and exporter of leather goods, chocolates, tobacco, cosmetics and ethnic jewelry.

Number 7

Merchant navy, navy and marine sciences and engineering, foreign services, exports, running traveling agencies, designer, predictor and counselor, social worker, writer, poet, art critic, sports correspondent, transcriptionist, journalist, dealer of white and silvery objects, psycho-analyst.

Number 8

Automobile engineering, mechanical engineering, surgery, research fellows in occult sciences, vastu consultants and future tellers, art criticism, philosophy, publishing, journalism, builders and contractors, writer, predictors, counselors, garage owners, transporters, vehicle manufacturing, can deal in iron- foundry works, petrol, automobiles, diamonds and black colored objects.

Number 9

Leader, politician, armed forces, martial arts, visual arts, judicial, administrative services, property dealing, mine– engineering, mining, publishing and printing, legal consultancy, spiritual mentors, photo journalists, social workers, developers, horticulturists, surgical instruments dealer, photography, movie-making, hotel management, diamond jewelry designer, business of multi-colored precious stones, dealer in arms and ammunition, cooking gas, fuel and agricultural products.

Chapter 17: Summary Of What To Expect From Your Number

In fact, let us not even confine ourselves to your singular number. What about that Life Path number for your son or daughter? How about that of your spouse? Do you not think it would do you a lot of good to, sort of, be able to predict what to expect of people close to you by understanding their Life Path numbers?

Of course you may have heard this: Everyone is unique so do not compare your kids… Alright – so they are. But how unique is each one of them? We are talking here of attributes that they cannot be said to have acquired or copied. In a great sense, therefore, it is a situation that calls for understanding and support for each member of your family.

Obviously some individuals are likely to feel bad about having been very impatient with people they love. That is, after understanding the information that numerology reveals. Luckily, it is never too late to learn.

Below is a quick recap of our Life Path numbers:

Number Ones

Prepare to see them take on automatic leadership and expect you all to follow. But you need not worry about performance – they go for excellence.

Number Twos

Consider yourself blessed to have such great friends who are sweet and very kind. But if you do not prod them into participation, they might as well remain like wallpaper: being seen but not heard.

Number Threes

If you thought you could ignore someone, it, definitely, is not among the Threes. These ones have great charisma and gain popularity very fast. Beware that this lot can persuade you into anything – possibly the lot we say can sell ice to the Eskimo…

So, be alert because, they could also be convincing in a way that leads you astray. Do not be surprised to catch them in a scam.

Number Fours

Do not get pissed off when you are with them in a team and they cannot spare a moment to have fun. That is their nature. They bury themselves in work and will not be settled till they are through. They are also too conscious of spending; so do not think they are being mean to you – they do not even lavish themselves; the reason many of them retire in relative comfort as compared to other people.

Number Fives

These people, whom we pointed out love their freedom, can sometimes be eccentric. They can even be ridiculously strange, doing things that go against accepted societal norms. So it would save you a lot of stress when living or working with such a person if you knew what to expect of them.

Number Sixes

If you want peace and normalcy, these are your guys. And do not worry – they are not boring. Things usually go well for them in life and so you need to be aware that they can appear to be a bit self-absorbed. Otherwise, they wish good things for everyone.

Number Sevens

Do not fear that they loathe you or your company just because they seem to choose to be alone. They are just deep thinkers who delve deep into issues in very high concentration. In fact, it would be advisable that you prompt them to share their wisdom with you and you see how valuable their knowledge can be.

Number Eights

If you are planning to have a personal relationship with an eight, be ready to go it alone sometimes because the eights' pursuit for wealth is overwhelming. And do not expect them to take responsibility for anything going wrong in that relationship as a result of their single-mindedness in pursuing wealth. In other words, when you receive no compassion from the Eights, try and take solace from knowing that you are not the problem – you know who is.

Number Nines

This very generous and romantic lot constitutes people who are selfless when it comes to safeguarding the rights of others. However, they could do with some directing, because, even with their good intentions, many times they fail to get their way round to making progress.

Number Eleven

Please do not go crazy when these people act as though they could level the world for everyone. That is just who they are – sometimes unrealistic. Maybe you could see how to tame them a bit and then let their intelligence help you reach high levels of achievement.

Number Twenty-two

How lucky could you be to have a Twenty-two in your team! They have the best of everyone else, from the ones to the elevens.

But beware – they can also be affected by the negative aspects of all the other numbers. In fact, there are instances when they turn out to be too manipulative and controlling.

Chapter 18: 9 Year Cycle

This is an interesting chapter, especially as I write this in 2017. As you will discover 2017 is a big year, numerically. Numerologists believe that time on Earth functions in 9 year cycles. Just how we worked our Life path number, we use a similar system to uncover the cycles which occur through the years. The main difference is that the 9-year cycle is the same for everyone. To calculate this, we only use the number of the year, in this case it is 2017. Add the single digits of the year together, then reduce it down to a single figure.

For example, if we take the year 2017 and 2018, it will reduce down to the number 1 and 2, respectively.

2017 = 2 + 0 + 1 + 7 = 10

1 + 0 = 1

2018 = 2 + 0 + 1 + 8 = 11

1 + 1 = 2

Using the above multiplication for each and every year, we will see a sequence emerging. For example, 2017 is reduced down to the number 1. 2018 reduced to the number 2, 2019 to the number 3 and so on. All the way to the year 2025 which becomes number 9. Then the same cycle will start over again. These cycles are on-going and are believed to hold significance to the whole of humanity.

With this understanding we can begin to see that 2016 was the end of a cycle and 2017 is a new beginning. Now we will look at each year individually (from 1-9) to see what each represents to us in terms of our growth and development.

Year 1

Understandably this is the year of new beginnings, it is about you and deciding what you want for the next 9 years. Due to a new cycle, we will naturally feel that we want change in our life. You may feel you want to get back into education, or find a new relationship or even start your own business. If nothing initially comes to mind, you will find out what you want as the year goes on, new ideas about change will automatically come to you. It is important to decide and plan for the next 9 years during year 1. It is also important to set goals in various areas of life and make the plans to achieve them. This year is about you and the decisions you need to make to direct your life. It is the foundation of the next 9-year cycle. Deciding on what you want and committing to it, makes year 1 the best year to create change. Here are some general questions we can ask ourselves to help prepare us for a new cycle.

What would you like more of in your life?

What parts of yourself are you happy to let go?

How would you like to treat yourself in the future?

How would you like to treat others? How will your relationships look?

What would you like achieve, gain or have?

Use these questions to uncover what you really want. You may already know what it is you want. Once you have decided, make the plans for their attainment.

Year 2

The second year of the cycle is mostly about partnerships, friendships and romance. Not just forming new relationships but also letting go of old ones. Usually a bad relationship will end during this year. We sometimes have to go with the flow and learn to let go sometimes. However, this is also the year of the Soulmate, so we are more likely to find a much healthier relationship, but not just in romance, we may find a new friend or business partner since this year is associated with union in all aspects. New opportunities can present themselves during year 2, it is also related to emotional health and balance. Year 2 is seen as a year of feminine energy.

Year 3

This year is related to moving forward with your career and achieving greater success. It is a positive year which brings happy vibrations. This is the year to make great progress on our goals. This year is also related to self-expression which will enable you to make new friends and become more sociable. Since this is an expansive year, a lot of the seeds you planted in years 1 and 2 will start to come to fruition. You may learn from new life experiences while also experiencing good fortune and seeing more money flowing into your life. You will generally have a lot of fun this year but remember to stay focused on your goals. Although this is a happy year, try to keep balanced because without it you may lose ground on longer-term goals.

Year 4

The fourth year of the cycle represents self-discipline and hard work. Here you may be required to dig deeper and to keep on pushing towards your dreams. The fun of Year 3 has passed and that is why it is important to keep on top of your goals during year 3. If we can leave year 3 in good shape, then we will be able to handle year 4 much better. With dogged determination however, we will start to see glimpses of our dreams manifesting in year 4. If however, we fall behind it can lead to a long and frustrating year. 4 is a grounded number, so you should try to maintain stability throughout.

Year 5

This has the potential to be a big year and if you have been building towards it with a solid plan and hard work then major change is on the cards. Aspects of your life whether it be career, finances, relationships or health will start to grow in positive ways. This year has the potential to bring adventure, excitement and more freedom than you have known before. These positive changes will enable you to live life at a higher level where you will find a new sense of stability. The primary symbol of year 5 is change. Since this is the central year of the 9 year cycle, it is our first real milestone to see how far we have come and if we are on track for our 9 year plan. This year is also related to health so it is important to stay on top of it.

Year 6

Year 6 is primarily concerned with our relationships in love, family and home life. Most of our intention and responsibility should be focused in this area as this is an emotional year for most. You may be required to make adjustments in your life. This can also involve healing past relationships which didn't work out as planned. It is not really a time for accomplishment but your progress towards your goals should be sustainable providing the groundwork and hard work over the last years was sufficient. Accept that this will be a slower and more personal year but should still bring you joy from your close relationships.

Year 7

As you move into year 7, you must begin to sustain any new relationships which were formed in year 6. This can lead to asking many questions about yourself. It can also involve emotional healing as you grow through your closet intimate relationships. For these reasons, it is a year where we learn a lot about ourselves and this requires much introspection. Maybe even taking a short trip away alone, to reflect on the past, has its benefits but also to look at your plans for the next 2 years of the cycle. Without deep introspection, we can fall into depression as we search for a deeper meaning and purpose to our life. This can also be a very spiritual year for many people, so you should allow yourself to be guided by your soul and intuition. 7 is a strong number for spiritual development, wisdom and development of oneself. Take care to use these 12 months wisely. Write, draw and express how you feel, which will help to integrate your thoughts. You may even uncover some new talents in year 7.

Year 8

This is the penultimate year before the end of the cycle. A big year for goal achieving and material attainment since this is a power year. You can make great progress towards your 9 year goals. Financially this is a great year also, you see the years of hard work finally paying off. In year 8 you will most likely experience your biggest achievements. Your potential will peak during this year so it is important to make the most of it. With a great year 8, it can set you up perfectly for the next 9-year cycle.

Year 9

The final year brings us to the end of this part of our life cycle. You should try to complete any unfinished business and let go off any negative relationships, tie up loose ends or release anything which doesn't serve you no-more. This enables us to step into the next cycle without the hindrance of things that we felt were dragging us down in the previous cycle. If we are hesitant to let some things go, we also prevent new opportunities coming our way. Slamming the door shut on certain things is more than necessary if we truly want change. This is the year to finally let things go. With these new insights, you will be more prepared and open to planning a better future.

Take the time to consider the last 9 years and see how far you have come and where you started from. If you are happy with the progress you made, acknowledge this and give yourself a metaphorical pat on the back. Feel proud of yourself, for making it through the 9-year cycle and the challenges you have overcome. It is a time of endings and new beginnings.

As previously mentioned, since this is being written in 2017, we are currently in the first year of a 9-year cycle, therefore our future plans can be made at any time during this year. The sooner the better of course. When we draw-up our plans for the next 9 years, the flow and energy of the cosmos aligns with us. These universal forces are primed for helping promote change and to encourage people to create what they want to see in their futures. If however, you are reading this book after 2017 and you haven't made any plans for this 9 year cycle. It is never too late, to start right now. We can achieve our goals and desires at any time, (as many people do) but working with the cycle gives us an extra push and helps us gain momentum quicker.

Synchronicity

This is a chapter on general synchronicity although numbers play a huge part in these types of messages, they can also come in different forms such as sounds and images. Sometimes we may think of something or someone and then coincidently we see that person or thing soon after. It really makes us think and can sometimes leave us speechless. We often say to ourselves, **'what are the chances of me seeing this person?'**. A deeper understanding of these coincidences, is the belief that what just occurred was not down to chance, but it was a synchronistic event that was intentional. This could be interpreted as a sign from the Universe, proving that everything is in divine order. The way to create more synchronistic events in life is to align your dominant thoughts with the direction your life is headed. For example, if you think about making more money (thoughts) and then take act through new ventures (action) to earn more money, your thoughts and actions are in alignment. This is a simple example, but this idea works for everything we are trying to achieve. Eventually through matching our behaviour and thinking, we attract more synchronistic events into our life. These occurrences send us encouragement and support to help us reach our goal.

Synchronicity – 'the simultaneous occurrence of events which appear significantly related but have no discernible causal connection' – **Oxford Dictionary**

In order to attract more synchronicity there a number of things we can do -

Visualize

Most of us don't use our minds to their full capability. Without knowing it we are attracting experiences into our lives every single day. Visualizing is a relatively simple technique, by using our imagination we can begin to experience more of what we want. Naturally this brings more synchronistic event to us. Once you decide what you want to do or achieve, the universe will send people, signs, numbers, messages and circumstances to you, for you to realize this desire. This happens when we want something badly enough, the universe pick-ups on our subtle vibration and responds by bringing things to us to help. Visualization of what you want is a sure-fire way of experiencing more synchronicity.

Be Aware

Synchronicity is happening around us every day, we just need to open our eyes and start to notice what is going on around us. This involves us being more present and conscious. Many people cannot see beyond physical reality, if they see a sign such as 11.11, they often pay it little attention. But by becoming more aware and alert, we can begin to notice everything significant that occurs around us. Once we start to notice signs, we open ourselves up to receive even more messages being sent to us. You can work on your degree of awareness by taking just 10-15 minutes each day to meditate. This will help to clear the mind and reduce any mental chatter. Both of which, stop us from receiving this divine wisdom.

Express Your Interests

Another method of experiencing more synchronicity is by expressing your interests out into the world. Whether that is online or in your local area. You can do this by joining meet-up groups or any type of online community which shares your interests. This will begin to draw more of what you want to you. You'll will meet more like-minded people. We sometimes have to put ourselves out there if we truly want to experience more of what we want. It can be scary sometimes, especially if it is new to us. But just by taking the steps to get out of your comfort zone, will bring more synchronistic events into your life.

Expect Synchronicity

Acknowledge every time you see a certain number or bump into a person who you had recently thought about. This is an important time to recognize it what has occurred as a synchronistic event. By doing this, we begin to draw more of these coincidences into our lives. Open yourself up to having these experiences, expect to see them every day. By setting the intention and having faith, this will bring more of these events into your lives.

Change Yourself

When we change or emotionally heal ourselves we start to align with our truth and who we really are. Synchronicity at a very basic level is balance and alignment. These magical events will only occur more often when everything is perfect harmony in that moment. By changing ourselves, we change our energetic vibration then everything starts to align with our new frequency. It has to, it is one of the laws of the Universe. If you are on the right path in life and developing into the person you want to be, then you will see signs such as 11.11 more often. You are in alignment with yourself and the Universe is affirming this to you.

Law of Attraction

You have probably heard popular phrase such as, 'like attracts like'. Science and specifically quantum physics has proven that we will attract to us, whatever vibration we put out. In other words, we get what we are by the frequency we project. This is how most people find their partners or friends. A matching of their energy vibration naturally draws them together. It is not an accident when we meet a certain person we feel a connection with, it is a universal law. We have been attracted to the other person magnetically through a synchronistic event. Having the knowledge of the type of person you are, will enable you to gain perspective on the type of person you will attract.

Timing

This requires you to have patience, which can be difficult for some of us. Just how the moon and the planets in our solar system work within a specific cycle and timing. The rising of the sun cannot be rushed. In a similar way, numbers are based upon cycles. We have to understand to trust the cycles and timing of our lives. What we want to see may not always occur as soon as we would like. Meditation is a great practice for helping us to build patience since we are not concerned with anything but the present moment.

All of the above-mentioned methods are great ways to put us into a natural flow with life and the Universe. Once we achieve this state, we open the door to more synchronistic events and allow great experiences to come into our lives. Whether that is the romantic partner you have been wishing for, a job or new a business opportunity, whatever it is, put yourself into the optimal state to be able to receive it. Take the time to practice these techniques and hopefully you too can enjoy some amazing circumstances. Remember to always keep your eyes peeled!

Chapter 19: Karmic Deficit Number:

Karmic number is your name and Karmic Deficit Number (KDN) is the vibrations missing in your name. Though the name of a person should be in tandem with his/her life path, if it fails to encompass all the vibrations of all the numbers 1 to 9, then you will inevitably have a Karmic Deficit Number in your name.

Thus it is important to note that the missing KDN will directly impact in any form and in any stage of your life, if it is part of your HOUSE number, VEHICLE number or even your MOBILE UMBER, the effect of the missing number will be felt. e.g. suppose a person's name is K Saseedaran Nair, you can have the KDN of this name by looking at the Pythagorean Numerology chart (see chapter -1) to determine what each alphabet denotes. For this example K(2), S(1), A(1), S(1), E(5), E(5), D(4), A(1), R(9), A(1), N(5), N(5), A(1),

I(9) and R(9), now let us look for the missing numbers which will tell us what vibrations are missing in this name and ofcourse this given example does not have the vibrations of number 3 (letter C, L, U), 4(Letter D, M, N), 6 (Letter F, O, X), 7(Letter G, P, Y), 8(Letter Q, L) so in this name KDN are 3, 4 6, 7, 8. So these five KDNs can influence this person anytime, anywhere without him realizing whenever there is direct or indirect contact with this deficit numbers.

This applies to a person when he/she drives a car. If the vehicle number/s is part of his/her KDN/numbers then the deficit number can form to incorporate into his/her character instantly. When this happens, then you can see a character change in his/her. This same principle apples when a person is using a mobile phone with certain Karmic Deficit Number/Numbers.

You House Number And you: certainly the house number you choose to rent or buy impact positively or otherwise on the people residing there and alphabets in the address need to be seen as numbers.

You ignore STREET names, i.e. your house is sited at Maple Leaf, avenue 2, it does not have any material impact. The unit number is crucial and if your unit is 23K, then ST you need to add, 2+3+the K(K has the power of 2), so we get 2+3+2=7.

People tend to rent/buy a house based on non-numerological facets like spaces, conveniences, whether it is bright with the morning sun; the direction that this main door faces; the proximity of neighbors and friends or because it was a good bargain.

This mode of reckoning applies also to the purchase of cars and if your car's number plate is SJC 217, then you need to add S(1)+ J(1)+ C(3)+2+1+7, which give us 15, which can be reduced to 6.

Mobile phone numbers, for the Chinese the addition of their personal mobile phone or residential phone numbers can affect them sentimentally and for e.g. if your mobile number is 5281 1377, then you add up all the numbers and in this case 5+2+8+1+1+3+7+7 gives us 34, which can be reduced to 7(3+4=7).

Some people even buy golden numbers adding up to the auspicious number 8 (Alluding to prosperity in Chinese) to bring the "CHI" (energy) to give the additional catalyst energy in their use of mobile phone numbers. But cannot be corrected.

Between a house and car, a house is far more import as a place of

Rest

Sleep

Bonding with family members

Rest and recreation

Now let us at the energy vibrations that each house would bring about.

House numbers/Their energy

Note: if certain number are a part of your KDN/s and if your house number has that particular deficit number, it will automatically affects you as explained earlier.

You need to remember it is NOT the house but the NUMBERS, that are living, breathing and responding to your vibrational frequency that achieve these quietly.

House Number 1 for Independent people

House Number 2 for Cooperation for peace and harmony

House Number 3 for creative outlet, for the arts, social parties

House Number 4 for Rules, Regulations like an army camp full of dos and don'ts

House Number 5 for change vitality, pro-business

House Number 6 for family-prone, friends and the arts and possibility

House Number 7 for Spirituality, peace, good for loners

House number 8 for Cognitive trade, magnet for money

House Number 9 for Completeness, humanitarian, spirituality and care

Why completeness? Because if you take any number and add to it, e.g. 9+5, you get 14, which can be reduced to 1+4=5 (The original number) or if you add 9+9, you get 18, which can be reduced to 1+8=9 (the original number again) and if you multiply ant number like 3X9, you get 27 and 2+7, you get 9 again and if you 8X9, you get 72 and 7+2 you get 9 again.

Note:Your Karmic Number (Your name is crucial in determining the energy that can be latent in your home and remember it is good to do a check on the MISSIG NUMBERS in your karmic number to find out the numbers that are absent. How to find out the missing numbers in your Karmic Numbers

Chapter 20: The Mercurial Temperament & Ultimate Salesman

Mercury and the number 5 are one. I refer to this number as the roller coaster, being more moody than the moon influenced 2, namely the 2, 11 and 20. In tropical astrology, the most common form used in the United States, Mercury in any chart denotes the individual's intellectual orientation or basic mental makeup. Those of you familiar with astrology are aware of the planet Mercury going forward and retrograde erratically and this pattern changes yearly thus reinforcing the term "mercurial disposition." A Mercury Birthday number is the mind, the intellect, and everything connected with thinking, regardless of whether you consider yourself an intellectual or not. A 5 Birthday's biggest challenge is dealing with mood swings, especially the sudden shift of melancholy that easily can turn into depression. Many 5s are of a fixed disposition. They like their personal space and environment to be their way, and they can use and turn this tendency inward to hold back any outward show of that mercurial temperament. A woman once told me that her 5 Birthday ex-boyfriend had many 4 tendencies. This is because 4 and 5 are both next to each other and the 5 is fixed and very physical like the 4 Birthday. The 5 may be moody but its nature is fixed. Watch against becoming too fixated on changing the world or trying to make a permanent imprint on things around you. In Sanskrit, Mercury is called "Buddha." **Buddha** is derivative of the planet's name. The Indian Sage by the same name who brought the form of enlightenment now known as Buddhism, initially used his meditation to ease his migraine headaches. A 5 needs to use his intelligence to improve his own lot.

Becoming obsessed with an idea, religion, or goal is another pitfall 5s need to watch for. This especially is true when the numerological chart has one or more 4, 5, or 8 Pinnacles. Sometimes they become fixated. I knew a young 5 Birthday woman who came from Paris to Los Angeles just to discover all she could about her idol Jim Morrison, the late singer for the rock band, The Doors. She wasn't content until she had found all of his known habitats. A 5 needs to use this moodiness to his benefit through artistic pursuits, sales or any other form of controlled roller coaster activity.

A 5 ruling any number cycle in one's life, is a good time to be in sales. If one isn't in sales, this also means a period of working on a contract basis. Adolf Hitler had a 5 Facade. He was among the best salespersons in history. He sold the Nazi party to millions of German voters. Combined with his 2 Birthday, he was the ultimate public relations man. Most people are aware that Hitler's 2/5 Birthday and Facade combined well enough towards public relations that he convinced a court in New York State to award him damages for an unauthorized English translation of his autobiography **Mein Kampf**. Jimmy Hoffa, the pivot of the Teamsters Union for decades was a 5 Birthday. Under his strong aggressive leadership, the Teamsters achieved their greatest gains, and they provided the example for the labor union movement during its zenith. Karl Marx, the ultimate scribe of Communism and Socialism, was of the proverbial mercurial temperament and most definitely obsessed with an idea.

One of my former history professors once claimed Marx's moodiness came from a lifelong skin problem that resulted in regular boils all over his body. I say this may have added to the problem, but Marx definitely held true to the mercurial temperament. Marx also came from a long line of rabbis. He may have been an avowed atheist, but his persistently dogmatic approach was as much, if not more adherent as that of any zealous religious leader. The extremely fixed and dogmatic policies of Marxist nations was not so much a fitting manifestation of Karl Marx's writings as they were a tribute to his 5 Birthday dogmatic nature. His idea of social evolution was very cut and dry. Marx envisioned a socialist society, followed by Communism, then ultimately a world of autonomous villages, towns and cities in an anarchistic society. His goal was disruption of the existing social order with what the corporate world might call an MBO (management by objectives).

5's romantic lives tend to be very promiscuous or like that of a monk, or it bounces between the two extremes. People's sex lives and relationship values come from a basic temperament as well as values. A Mercury Birthday's promiscuity merely would be a manifestation of his moodiness. A 2/5 romantic relationship is one I wouldn't recommend. The initial attraction might center on the immediate sexual gratification and the all-around good times on the first few dates but this attraction could turn sour, especially if the 2 is a female. After that time frame, the same attraction begins to wear the 2's nerves thin.

A 2 and 5 Birthday would have a roller coaster time with emotional conflict and finances, though for the latter, their combined luck would be their redeeming quality at the last moment. A 3/5 romance would have much sexual energy, but there might be problems with fidelity, especially if the man is the 5. A 4/5 romance is another very physical affair. Make sure that the 4's anger doesn't turn the relationship into a battle zone. This relationship works well with either sex being the 5. A pair of 5s might make it as friends, but these numbers are at odds with each other. Their moodiness would not provide healthy friction; it merely would collide.

Chapter 21: If You Born On The 7 (Seventh) Or 16th (Sixteen Or 25th (Twenty Fifth) Of Any Month Than Kindly Read The Following:

THE NUMBER SEVENS

In general, those with a seven birth date are unusual people with special talents. Intellectual and absorbed, they are often considered loner and lover of solitude. They generally love nature, animals, and serene environments.

Material success means less to them than being able to live life by their own rules. By nature they are deep peoples, intuitive and observant with spiritual and technical abilities. Seven are usually cautious and move very slowly when making decisions. Alcoholism is sometime a problem for sevens. They do not take advice well. You will succeed if you will learn to concentrate on one thing at a time. Your intuition will lead you to the right opportunities and then you have to get specialized training in the field you have chosen. You may have fine technical abilities. Your work may involve a great deal of research or you may be a farmer or a rancher, immersed in the land.

You tend to follow your hunches rather than someone else advise. You should realize that you have strong opinion that you may not want to compromise, and relationships may suffer from your intractability.

You will find your opportunities coming to you though patient waiting; if you try to be aggressive, you may experience frustration at the pace of events. Never gamble. Your attitude of caution in regard to money is correct. You may play an esoteric instrument or have unusual hobbies and friends. You have an affinity for the country and animals, and meditation and solitude are absolute necessities for you.

You may be prone to be quite and have few special friends rather than many.

You like to spend time alone but have to be careful not to become too withdrawn. You need to meditate and do some spiritual exercise in order to develop your intuitive talents. You have par excellence intuition. Once you have begun to trust your intuition, you would have a sound faith

You prefer to work alone and set your own pace. You tend to finish projects once started. Your interest leans to the scientific, technical, and metaphysical effects of life. You are quite sensitive and feel deeply involved, in everything but you don't share your feelings that easily and tend not to communicate them to anyone. At times you can be stubborn. You can be highly critical and self-centered these trends can lead to unhappiness, if you are not careful.

You should specialize in one given field in order to make full use of your caliber and abilities and your natural intellectual talent.

IF YOU WERE BORN ON THE 16th

Yours is one of the most unusual birthday number. It bring startling events which become turning point in your life. Your friends will be highly unusual. You may chose an eccentric lifestyle and always have a feeling that you are somehow different. The 16 is a karmic number.

This may mean that you have connections with people based on past life experiences and you will feel a special quality when you meet them-or by the way you meet them. Life is never dull with the 16. Many things are learned the hard way. You do not take undue risks. Your attitude may complicate your working or marital situations. Because of the nature slowness of the Sevens, you may procrastinate. You are analytic and may pursue technical or historical fields.

You may uncover facts of great significance or invent something entirely new. You insist that friends be of high quality. You may love antiques and stamp collections. You consider love as the most beautiful thing and you love to fall in love, but a number of your group members think that the person they love is not sincere with them. You love to be with your friends and you are always found to be a dutiful friend. You can hardly control your patience, which is a very big drawback of your nature. Gives a sense of loneliness and generally the desire to work alone. You are relatively inflexible, and insist on your being independent.

You need a good deal of time to rest and to meditate. You are introspective and a little stubborn. Because of this, it may not be easy for you to maintain permanent relationships, but you probably will as you are very much into home and family. They have got the strong tendencies of exploring the hidden meaning behind situations and circumstances. You are considered to be very knowledgeable and your intellectual level is very high. You are known for taking wise decisions and are very good in researches. The only problem with you are with is that you keep most of the knowledge to yourself. That's where you need to get improved. The knowledge and learning gets better when you share it with others. Let you be known for your intellectual achievements and ideas rather than to keep them as a secret.

Share your perspective with others. This will make this earth planet a better place to live in. Secrecy beyond a level doesn't help you in achieving anything in life. Nor does you allow success in your love. Even though you try hard you find it difficult to hold on to your lover. The love melts and slips through your life.

You are more interested in the occult. You gain knowledge in, numerology, astrology and occult sciences. You research into religion and spirituality. You believe in simple living and high thinking. This unique number 16 says that even if you make money you do not enjoy your riches. You think that others around you lead a false life. You want to guide them to your path of purity and simplicity. Your birth number sixteen inclines to interests in the technical, the scientific, and to the religious explorations.

Conclusion

We often feel the pressures of life when we don't take time to discover what the universe has in store for us, so we take on this journey thinking we can do it all and get stuck along the way. The objective of this book is to help you strike a connection between your life and astrology, and we have achieved more than that thus far.

Don't try to walk alone when you can get help from the supreme universe through the concept of astrology, don't try to "Take a guess" at what will work or fail all on your own when you have a system that perfectly aligns your emotions, feelings, thoughts, and circumstances together.

Astrology empowers you to take the reins of your life and tackle your own journey with the assurance of getting impressive results. This has been an inspiring journey thus but there is a crucial concept we must discuss as we round off, it borders on the idea of sustainability.

Information on astrology is replete all over the internet, books, podcasts, etc. with the comprehensive details you've received through this book (as will other people) one can only wonder why people still make the same relationship, financial and life mistakes that they experience.

The reason for their inability to translate what they learn into their lives is because they lack a sustainable approach to learning. After putting this book down so many people will get excited and try out the astrology for a few days, okay maybe a few weeks and then boom! They completely forget about it!

Two years down the road, they will hear someone speak of the positive effect of astrology, and they will say "Oh I used to practice that but not anymore" this is not the way to go when knowledge is acquired. There are three things you should note:

1. Learning
2. Doing
3. Sustaining

So you just completed the first step, you've learned so much about astrology, but you must take the next level by actually doing something with what you've learned. After that, you should start thinking about sustaining it all long-term because that is how it will become a part of your life.

Astrology is not a passive idea, and when you don't take action with it, you will be depriving yourself of the opportunity to add value to your life through the lessons learned.

As we round off this experience here, get excited about the idea of sustainability by actively taking steps towards using astrology in your unique experience. The words in this book should transcend the pages and come alive with your finances, relationships, friendships and every other area of your life.

The question you should be asking yourself at this point is "What am I going to do with the vital lessons gained?" use it, continue with it and let your astrological success story inspires others to do the same.

It's a whole new world now as you harness the potentials of astrology and bask in the feeling of taking control of your life. Ready to strike a secure connection with the universe?

Start implementing, take action, and enjoy the process!

www.ingramcontent.com/pod-product-compliance
Lightning Source LLC
Chambersburg PA
CBHW072008070526
44583CB00015B/1385